10 MINUTE GUIDE TO Lotus Organizer™

Robert Mullen

alpha books

A Division of Prentice Hall Computer Publishing
201 West 103rd Street, Indianapolis, Indiana 46290 USA

To my mom, Cecile Label, to whom I'll always be the consummate beginner.

©1994 Alpha Books

All rights reserved. No part of this book shall be reproduced, stored in a retrieval system, or transmitted by any means, electronic, mechanical, photocopying, recording, or otherwise, without written permission from the publisher. No patent liability is assumed with respect to the use of the information contained herein. Although every precaution has been taken in the preparation of this book, the publisher and author assume no responsibility for errors or omissions. Neither is any liability assumed for damages resulting from the use of the information contained herein. For information, address Alpha Books, 201 W. 103rd Street, Indianapolis, IN 46290.

International Standard Book Number:1-56761-458-2
Library of Congress Catalog Card Number: 93-74245

96 95 94   8 7 6 5 4 3 2

Interpretation of the printing code: the rightmost number of the first series of numbers is the year of the book's printing; the rightmost number of the second series of numbers is the number of the book's printing. For example, a printing code of 94-1 shows that the first printing of the book occurred in 1994.

Screen reproductions in this book were created by means of the program Collage Plus from Inner Media, Inc., Hollis, NH.

Printed in the United States of America

Publisher
Marie Butler-Knight

Managing Editor
Elizabeth Keaffaber

Development Editor
Kelly Oliver

Production Editor
Michelle Shaw

Copy Editor
SanDee Phillips

Book Designer
Roger Morgan

Indexer
Craig Small

Production Team
Gary Adair, Katy Bodenmiller, Brad Chinn, Kim Cofer, Meshell Dinn, Mark Enochs, Stephanie Gregory, Jenny Kucera, Beth Rago, Marc Shecter, Greg Simsic, Carol Stamile

Special thanks to C. Herbert Feltner for ensuring the technical accuracy of this book.

Contents

1 Starting and Exiting Organizer, 1

Starting Lotus Organizer, 1
Understanding the Parts of the Screen, 2
About Organizer's Sections, 4
Quitting Lotus Organizer, 5

2 Using SmartIcons, 7

What Are SmartIcons?, 7
The SmartIcon Palette, 8
Changing the Position of the Palette, 9

3 Getting Help, 11

Using Organizer's On-Line Help, 11
The Help Menu, 12
Searching for Help on a Specific Topic, 13

4 Creating, Opening, and Saving Files, 16

Creating a New Organizer File, 16
Saving an Organizer File, 16
Saving Another Copy of an
 Organizer File, 17
Opening an Existing Organizer File, 18
Combining Organizer Files, 20

5 Moving Around in the Calendar, 23

Looking at the Calendar, 23
Changing the View of the
 Appointment Pages, 25
Changing Pages, 25

6 Scheduling Appointments with the Calendar, 27

Making an Appointment, 27
Editing Text in an Appointment, 28
Changing the Day of an Appointment, 29
Deleting an Appointment, 30

7 Using the TimeTracker to Adjust Appointments, 32

What Is the TimeTracker?, 32
Changing the Length of an
   Appointment, 33
Changing the Time of an Appointment, 34

8 Adding Extras to Your Appointments, 36

Using the Options in the
   Appointment Window, 36
Setting Alarms, 36
Running Applications at a Preset Time, 38
Associating Costs to Appointments, 39

9 Setting Calendar Preferences, 42

Customizing Your Calendar, 42
Displaying Information
   from Other Sections, 45

10 Working with the To Do List, 47

What Is the To Do List?, 47
Adding Tasks to the To Do List, 47
Managing Items, 50
Removing Items from the To Do List, 51

11 Using the Notepad to Make a Note for Yourself, 53

What Is the Notepad?, 53
Making Notepad Pages, 53
Looking at a Notepad's
   Table of Contents, 57
Pasting into a Notepad Page, 58
Deleting Notepad Pages, 59

12 Working with the Planner, 60

What Is the Planner?, 60
Changing Your View of the Planner, 61

Adding Events, 63
Using the Planner with the Calendar, 64

13 Setting Up the Address Section, 66

Using the Address Section, 66
Changing Address Views, 67
Adding an Address, 68
Changing an Address, 69
Deleting an Address, 70

14 Working with the Address Section, 71

Finding an Address, 71
Changing the Sort Order, 72

15 Importing and Exporting Addresses, 74

Importing Addresses, 74
Exporting Addresses, 77

16 Logging and Tracking Phone Calls, 80

Logging a Call, 80
Tracking Phone Calls, 83

17 Working with Anniversaries, 86

What Is an Anniversary?, 86
Adding an Anniversary, 87
Changing an Anniversary, 88
Deleting an Anniversary, 89

18 Printing, 91

Printing Sections of the Organizer, 91
Printing Labels, 94

19 Customizing Page Layout, 96

Choosing a Page Layout, 96
Changing the Page Setup, 97
Selecting a Font, 99

20 Using a Password, 102

Establishing a Password, 102
Changing a Password, 103

21 Customizing Organizer, 106

Putting Your Name on Your Organizer, 106
Changing the Color of the Binder, 106
Setting Display Preferences, 107

22 Using the Autodialer, 111

What Is the Autodialer?, 111
Making a Phone Call, 111
Reviewing the Phone Log, 113
Setting Autodialer Preferences, 115

23 Using Links to Cross Reference Information, 117

What Are Links? , 117
Setting Up Links , 118
Using Multiple Links, 120
Using Information
   from Other Applications, 122

24 Using Organizer Utilities, 125

What Are the Organizer Utilities?, 125
Saving a Damaged File, 125
Compacting a File, 127

A Windows Basics, 129

Tell Me About Windows, 129
Starting Microsoft Windows, 129
Parts of a Windows Screen, 130
Using a Mouse, 131
Starting a Program, 132
Using Menus, 132
Navigating Dialog Boxes, 133
Switching Between Windows, 135
Controlling A Window, 135

Index, 137

Introduction

It begins like this. Your boss calls reminding you to attend an important meeting tomorrow. You frantically look around for the minutes to that last meeting with your boss, and suddenly realize the cleaning people must have discarded them. They were in that cardboard box under your desk—you know, the one where you keep notes to yourself, records of phone conversations, and the minutes of important meetings. You panic.

If that's not bad enough, the phone rings. An important vendor is calling you from the lobby to announce that he's here—right on time—and ready to meet with you. You can't remember making the appointment, but apparently you did. The vendor has shown up with critical materials, and the production lines will go down if someone doesn't meet with him immediately.

The day ends like this: Your mom calls you at the office to apologize for forgetting your wedding anniversary. Oh no! What's the date today?! Where's that Post-It note that was supposed to remind you about your anniversary? Now you can't even go home!

It's time to get off the paper train. You need the *10 Minute Guide to Lotus Organizer*.

What Is Organizer?

Lotus Organizer is a popular *Personal Information Management* (or PIM) application designed for use with Microsoft Windows. Lotus Organizer helps you keep your daily life organized.

This book teaches you only what you need to know in order to get productive fast with Lotus Organizer. You can learn how to:

- Schedule appointments and meetings
- Keep track of special dates and events
- Make notes to yourself
- Manage a name and address list
- Print labels and pages suited for your loose-leaf organizer
- Create and maintain a To Do list

Organizer lets you combine information from different sources, such as your favorite spreadsheet or database. You can export Organizer's information in popular file formats, such as dBASE. You can link data from other applications while they're running to keep the information in your Organizer files current.

Organizer is not a tool that you lug around with you. It's a computerized way to coordinate information that's really important to you. Organizer helps you keep track of all that stuff you used to keep in your head (with marginal success). After all, no one can remember absolutely everything!

How to Use the Ten Minute Guide

Each of the short lessons in this Guide include step-by-step instructions for performing some specific task. The following special icons are included as a way to help you quickly identify particular types of information:

Introduction   xi

Plain English icons appear wherever a new term is defined. Watch for this symbol to help you learn the terms you'll need to understand Lotus Organizer and to learn more about how it works.

Panic Button icons appear next to areas where new users might run into trouble. Watch for this symbol to help you avoid making mistakes.

Timesaver Tip icons draw your attention to short-cuts and hints on how to use the ideas presented most effectively. Watch for this symbol to identify ways to save time when using Lotus Organizer.

Conventions Used in This Book

To help you quickly move through the lessons, these conventions are used:

What you type	Information you must type appears in bold, color type.
Items you select	Items you select or keys you press appear in color type.
On-screen text	Messages that display on your screen appear in a bold type.

Shortcut keys   Shortcut keys for select-
                            ing menu items and
                            commands appear in bold
                            color. In this book, the
                            boldface letter (selection
                            letter) corresponds to the
                            underlined letter you see
                            on-screen. Use these keys
                            to select items with the
                            keyboard instead of the
                            mouse.

Key combinations   In many cases, you must
                            press a two-key combi-
                            nation in order to enter
                            a command. For ex-
                            ample, "Press Alt+X." In
                            such cases, hold down
                            the first key and press
                            the second key.

Acknowledgments

Special thanks to Matt Wagner for making the *Ten Minute Guide to Lotus Organizer* a reality for me and to Kelly Oliver at Alpha Books for her guidance and understanding throughout this project.

Trademarks

All terms mentioned in this book that are known to be trademarks or service marks are listed below. In addition, terms suspected of being trademarks or service marks have been appropriately capitalized. Alpha Books cannot attest to the accuracy of this information. Use of a term in this book should not be regarded as affecting the validity of any trademark or service mark.

dBASE is a registered trademark of Borland International Incorporated.

Lotus 1-2-3, Lotus Organizer, and Lotus SmartSuite are registered trademarks of Lotus Development Corporation.

MS-DOS and Windows are trademarks of Microsoft Corporation.

Rolodex is a registered trademark of Rolodex Corporation.

Lesson 1

Starting and Exiting Organizer

In this lesson, you'll learn how to start and exit Lotus Organizer. You'll also learn about the different parts of Organizer's screen.

Starting Lotus Organizer

Before you can start Lotus Organizer, you must have Windows running. If you haven't yet started Windows, you'll need to do so by typing **WIN** at the DOS prompt.

> **Error Message!** If you get an error message, such as **Bad command or file name** when you type **WIN**, that means that you don't have the Windows directory in your DOS path statement. To switch to the Windows directory, type **cd\windows** and press Enter. To start Windows, type **WIN** and press Enter.

When you start Windows, you should have the Program Manager window on-screen. If you aren't sure whether the window on your screen is the right one, check the title bar. If it says **Program Manager**, then you're all set. If you have a Program Manager icon at the bottom of your screen instead of a window, double-click on the icon. It will open into a window.

What About Windows? To learn about basic Windows navigation, check out the Windows Primer in the back of this book.

Here's how you start Lotus Organizer from Program Manager:

1. Double-click on the Lotus Applications program group icon. The Lotus Applications group window opens (see Figure 1.1).

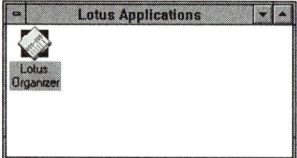

Figure 1.1 The Lotus Applications group window.

Where's the Icon? If the Lotus Applications icon isn't showing on-screen, you can use Program Manager's **W**indow menu to select it. Just click on the **W**indow menu, then click on Lotus Applications.

2. Double-click on the **Lotus Organizer** icon to start the program.

Understanding the Parts of the Screen

Lotus Organizer has one of the simplest and most easily understood screens of any software product for the personal computer. Organizer's application window is made up of all of the usual Windows screen objects, such as the Control-menu box, the title bar, Minimize/Maximize buttons, window borders, and Organizer's menu bar. Figure 1.2 shows you the Organizer application window and the parts of its screen.

Starting and Exiting Organizer 3

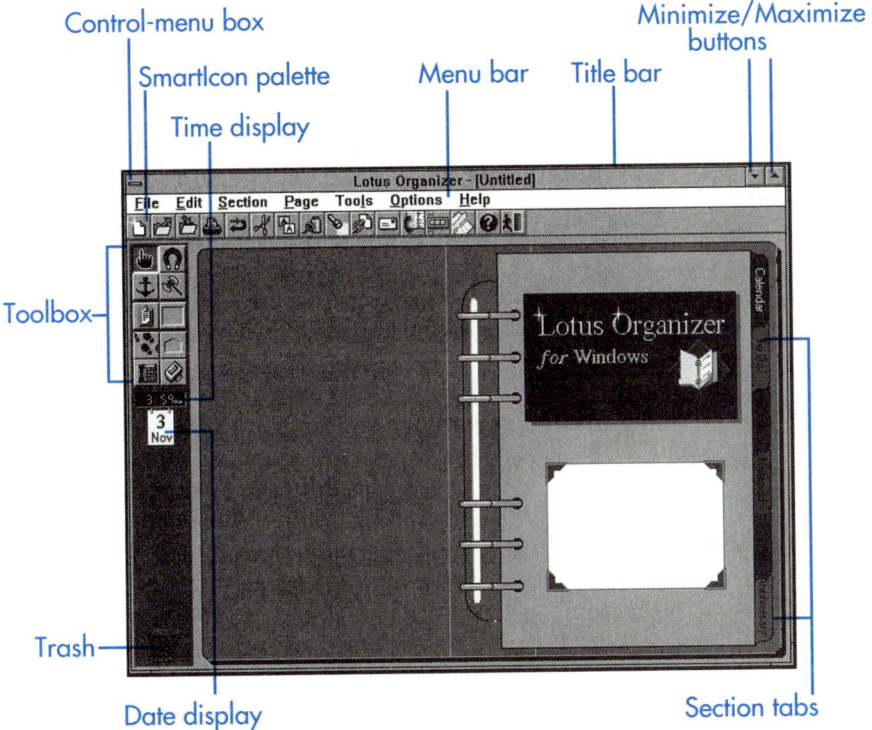

Figure 1.2 Organizer's screen.

Here are the main parts of Organizer's screen:

- SmartIcons are arranged in a horizontal strip, spanning from the left side of the screen to the right, called the *SmartIcon palette.* You click on a SmartIcon to run a commonly used task, like opening or saving a file. SmartIcons save you steps by helping you avoid making several menu selections. (Check out Lesson 2 for more on SmartIcons.)

- The *Toolbox* holds up to 17 buttons that let you change the pointer, link information, turn to the previous page in the current section, send/receive mail, make phone calls, print information, and so on. To learn what a Toolbox button does, point to it and hold down the right mouse button.

- The *Time Display* shows the time maintained by your computer system.

- Click on *Today's Date*, and the section that is currently open will reveal the pages for today's date.

- There are four icons that make up the *View icon palette*. These icons will appear only if you are using the Address section. Use them to change the way pages are displayed.

- You can drag information into the *Trash* from any of the six sections. When you drag-and-drop text into the Trash, it goes up in "flames."

- The *section tabs* are found along the right or left side of the binder (depending on the view). Each of these section tabs represents a section, such as the Address or the Calendar. Click on a tab to switch to that tab's section.

About Organizer's Sections

Organizer is made up of six sections. Each section performs a different task. If you use a daily planner now, you're probably familiar with these six sections:

- **Calendar**   Keeps track of important dates.
- **To Do**   Organizes what you do and when you do it.
- **Address**   Records addresses and phone numbers.
- **Notepad**   An electronic pad of paper.
- **Planner**   Organizes related events and people.
- **Anniversary**   Remembers important dates.

Organizer treats these sections as separate documents within a single file. Each single file is called an Organizer file. You can create and maintain as many Organizer files as your

Starting and Exiting Organizer 5

hard drive can handle, but you can only work with one at a time. Most die-hard Organizer users keep separate Organizer files for work, home, or activity lifestyles.

Quitting Lotus Organizer

You can quit Lotus Organizer in one of three ways (see Figure 1.3):

- Double-click on the Control-menu box.
- Select Exit from Organizer's File menu.
- Click on the Exit SmartIcon.

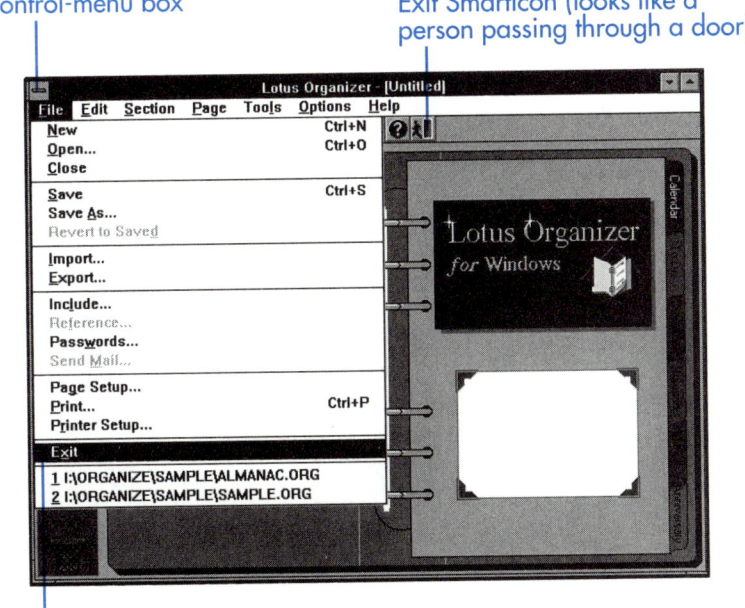

Figure 1.3 Three ways to exit Organizer.

It's important to leave the application in one of these three ways so that Organizer has the chance to save any new or changed information. If any files are open and unsaved,

Lotus Organizer will prompt you to do so with the Save As dialog box. For more information about saving files, turn to Lesson 4.

In this lesson, you learned how to start and exit Organizer. You also learned about the parts of Organizer's screen. In the next lesson, you'll learn about Organizer's SmartIcons.

Lesson 2

Using SmartIcons

In this lesson, you'll learn about Organizer's SmartIcons.

What Are SmartIcons?

SmartIcons act like push-buttons. When you click on a SmartIcon, the task that button represents is carried out. For example, when you click on the **Save** SmartIcon, the currently active file is saved. Because you don't have to use the menu system, SmartIcons minimize the steps needed to complete a common task.

Organizer is configured with several SmartIcons that are arranged on its SmartIcon palette. Table 2.1 shows you the SmartIcons.

Table 2.1 Organizer's SmartIcons

SmartIcon	Description
	Create a new file
	Open a previously saved file
	Save the currently active file
	Print the active document

continues

Table 2.1 Continued

SmartIcon	Description
	Undo the last action
	Cut data to the Clipboard
	Copy data to the Clipboard
	Paste data from the Clipboard
	Search for information
	Link files
	Send mail
	View the phone log
	Floating SmartIcons
	Customize a section
	Help
	Exit

The SmartIcon Palette

Most of the popular SmartIcons are installed in the *current palette*. The current palette, which is the one shown in Figure 2.1, is automatically used the first time you start Organizer.

Using SmartIcons   9

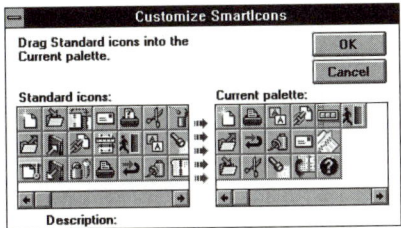

Figure 2.1   The current SmartIcon palette.

Changing the Position of the Palette

You can change the way Organizer displays its palette of SmartIcons. You can position the palette along the top, bottom, left side, or right side of Organizer's screen. You can make SmartIcons display in an unattached, or *floating*, position. You can even position SmartIcons out of sight if you want.

> **Floating Palette**   If the SmartIcon palette is floating, that means it is in its own window rather than being anchored on an edge of the screen. You can move the floating window around on-screen by dragging its title bar, and you can resize the window by dragging its borders.

Here's how you reposition the display of the SmartIcon palette:

1. Select SmartIcons from the Tools menu. The Tools SmartIcons dialog box will open, as shown in Figure 2.2. As you can see, the default position is the Top of Organizer's screen.

Lesson 2

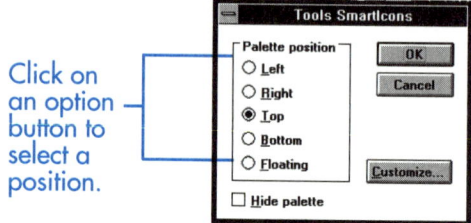

Figure 2.2 The Tools SmartIcons dialog box.

2. Click on one of the option buttons to select the palette position.

3. If you don't want to use the SmartIcon palette, you can click on the Hide palette check box to keep SmartIcons from being displayed.

4. Click on the OK button to close the Tools SmartIcons dialog box and reposition your SmartIcons.

In this lesson, you learned about Organizer's SmartIcons, and you learned how to reposition the SmartIcon palette. In the next lesson, you will learn how to get help from Organizer when you need it.

Lesson 3

Getting Help

In this lesson, you'll learn about using Organizer's help system.

Using Organizer's On-Line Help

Organizer has a comprehensive help facility that can be accessed by simply pressing the F1 key (or by clicking on the Help SmartIcon) at any time. Lotus Organizer's Help is context-sensitive, which means that pressing F1 gives you a Help window for the task you are currently trying to accomplish.

Context Sensitive A kind of Help that, when you ask for it, knows what you're doing and gives you very specific information. For example, if you press F1 while the Save As dialog box is on-screen, you get help on saving files.

Lotus Organizer also has a type of Help that's similar to the Help system used on Macintosh computers. On a Mac, it's called Balloon Help; Organizer calls it *Bubble help*. To use it, simply use the mouse pointer to select the object of interest, then press and hold the right mouse button while you read the text in the bubble. Bubble help is the fastest, simplest, and easiest way to learn about something you see on your screen. Figure 3.1 shows you Bubble help for the **Help** SmartIcon.

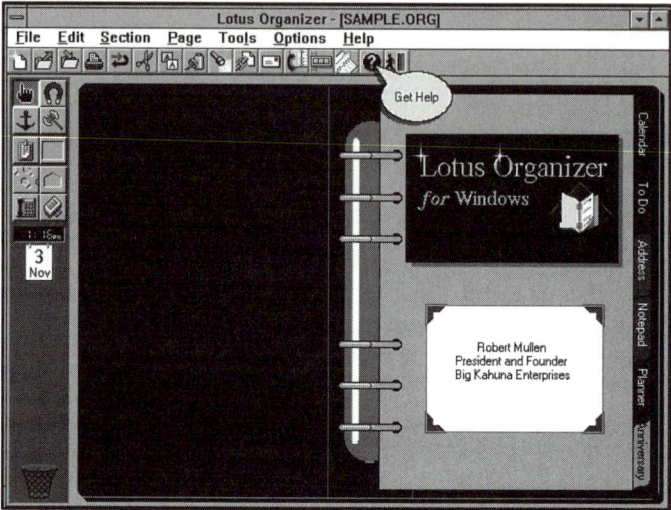

Figure 3.1 An example of Bubble Help.

The Help Menu

Although context-sensitive Help is often handy, sometimes you might need help on a topic that is not related to what is currently on-screen. In that case, you can use the **Help** menu, found on the main menu bar.

Organizer's **Help** menu makes six menu items available to you. They are:

- **Index**—Provides you with a list from which to select more specific Help. When you select **Index** from Organizer's **Help** menu, a Help window opens to show you a list of ten *jump words* that, when clicked upon, display Help text specific to that jump word.

Getting Help   13

Jump Word   Words that cause more specific Help text to appear when clicked upon. Jump words are usually denoted by the use of green text. Click on a green jump word to learn more about the topic represented by that jump word.

- **How Do I?**—Opens a window that displays a list of common tasks performed with Lotus Organizer. Click on any of the items displayed to learn more about performing the selected task.

- **Commands**—Provides you with a description of the function for each of Organizer's main menu items and the items found on each main menu.

- **Shortcuts**—Helps you learn faster ways to run Organizer. You can learn about keyboard or mouse shortcuts.

- **Using Help**—Teaches you how to use Organizer's Help facility. You'll learn how to get help from anywhere in Organizer.

- **About Organizer**—Shows you information about the application and your copy of it.

Searching for Help on a Specific Topic

The Search feature will find the most specific Help text related to a topic of your choosing. You can Search for specific help by clicking on the Search button when using Organizer's Help system.

Here's how you can search for Help on a specific topic:

1. Press the F1 key, click on any Help button, click on the Help SmartIcon, or select any item from the Help menu. The Help window will open, shown in Figure 3.2.

14 Lesson 3

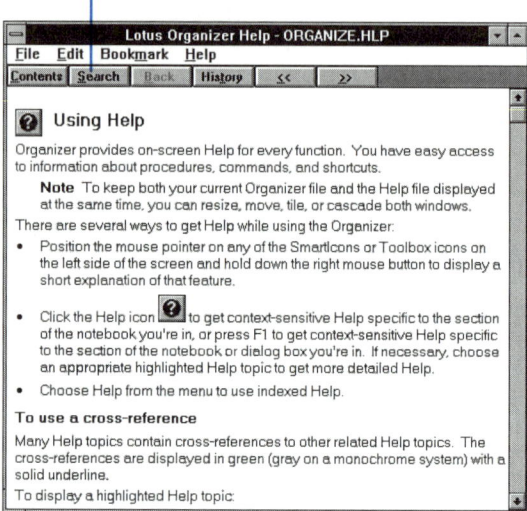

Figure 3.2 The Search button.

2. Click on the Search button. The Search dialog box will open, shown in Figure 3.3.

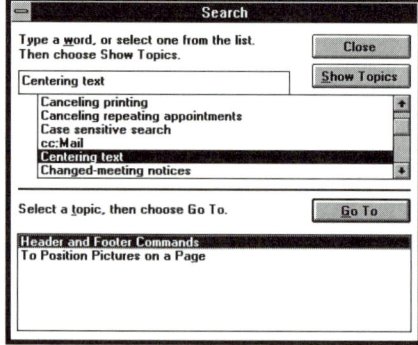

Figure 3.3 The Search dialog box.

Creating, Opening, and Saving Files

3. Click on the section you want to add.

4. Click on the Include button. A new dialog box, like the one in Figure 4.4, will open.

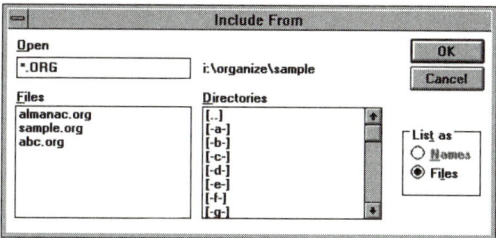

Figure 4.4 The Include From dialog box.

5. In the appropriate list boxes, select the drive, directory, and file name of the file that's supplying the information.

6. Click on the OK button. The Include Section dialog box, shown in Figure 4.5, will open.

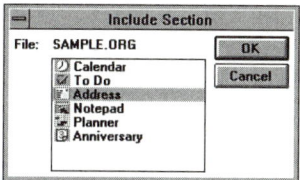

Figure 4.5 The Include Section dialog box.

7. Select a section to be included, and click on the OK button. The Include Section dialog box will close, revealing the Customize Organizer dialog box once again.

8. If you want to add any more sections, click on the Include button and repeat steps 3–7. If not, click on the OK button to close the Customize Organizer dialog box.

In this lesson, you learned how to create, save, open, and combine Organizer files. In the next lesson, you'll learn how to navigate through the Calendar.

Lesson 5

Moving Around in the Calendar

In this lesson, you'll learn how to navigate the Calendar section of Organizer.

Looking at the Calendar

The Calendar works just like the calendar you have sitting on your desk or hanging on your wall. You simply turn to the page you want to look at, and write down appointments and other things you don't want to forget. An advantage to using an electronic calendar is that you never have to cross off, white-out, or erase appointments that were rescheduled or cancelled. You can just move the appointment to a new date or time, or delete it altogether. (For information on changing appointments, turn to Lesson 6.)

To open the Calendar, click on the Calendar tab. The Calendar will open to a page showing all the months of the current year. There will be a red square around today's date, as shown in Figure 5.1.

Lesson 5

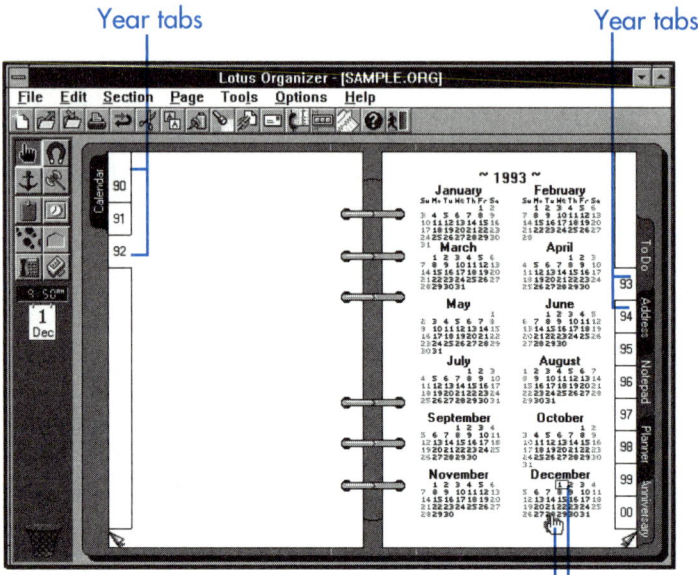

The mouse pointer is shaped like a hand when positioned on a date.

Today's date has a box around it.

Figure 5.1 The first page of the Calendar shows the months of the current year.

To open the Calendar to a certain date, just click on it. If you want to go to a date in a different year, you can click on the appropriate year tab. When you click on a date, the Calendar opens to that date's appointment page. If you click on the name of a month, the Calendar will open to the first day of that month.

> **Turn to Today** The fastest way to find today's date in the Calendar is to click on the Date display. (The Date display is below the Toolbox. It looks like a small calendar page.)

Changing the View of the Appointment Pages

When you're in the Calendar, there are four different ways you can display the dates on the page. Organizer calls these ways *views*. Each view is represented by an icon that is located beneath the Toolbox. The icons and their descriptions are shown in Table 5.1

Table 5.1 View icons

Icon	Description
	One day per page
	One work week per two pages
	One calendar week per two pages
	One calendar week per page

Calendar's default view is to show one calendar week on two pages. If you need more or less space for each date displayed, change your view of the page. Simply click on one of the four view icons.

Organizer's Calendar section remembers the view you like. When you open that same file again, you'll notice that Calendar displays the page in the last view you selected.

Changing Pages

You can look into the near future or the recent past by flipping through the pages of your Calendar. When you're looking for a page just a few days away, you can use your mouse to quickly turn to it.

Look at the lower-outside edge of the pages of the Calendar. You'll see that each page looks like it's turned back a little. All you have to do is click on these lower-outside page corners to turn the page. Take a quick look at Figure 5.2 to find these page corners.

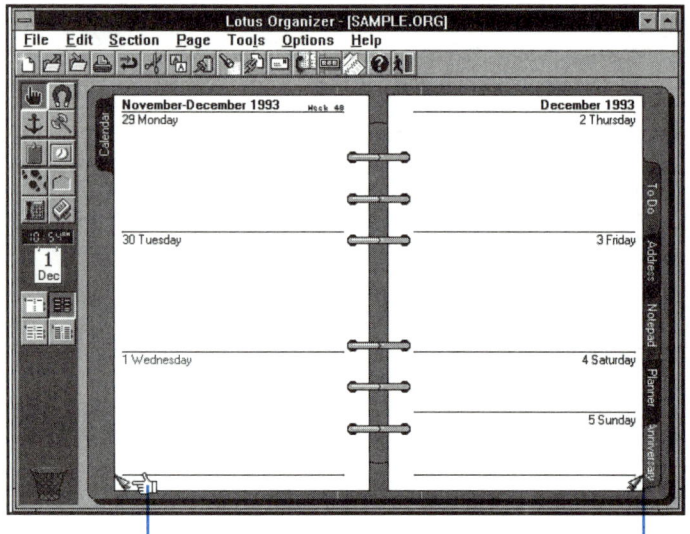

The mouse pointer changes to a hand when positioned correctly.

Turned back page corner

Figure 5.2 Turning to another page of the Calendar.

If you want to turn to a page in a different month or a different year, click on the Calendar section tab again. You'll be returned to the first page of the current year's calendar, where you can select a new year or a new date.

In this lesson, you learned how to move about within the Calendar. In the next lesson, you'll learn how to schedule and work with appointments.

Lesson 6

Scheduling Appointments with the Calendar

In this lesson, you'll learn how to schedule, edit, and delete appointments with Organizer's Calendar section.

Making an Appointment

If you work with people, you probably have to juggle commitments and accommodate scheduling conflicts in order to get together with them successfully. Lotus Organizer lets you schedule new appointments easily.

Here's how you make new appointments with Organizer:

1. Click on the Calendar tab to activate the Calendar.

2. If necessary, click on the year tab of the appropriate year.

3. Select a day for the new appointment by clicking on it.

4. Select a view by clicking on one of the view icons located below the Toolbox.

5. Click on the white space under the date of the day you want to use for your appointment.

6. In the vertical list that appears, click on a time slot. Use the scroll bar to find the preferred time slot if it isn't visible. The appointment window, as shown in Figure 6.1, will appear.

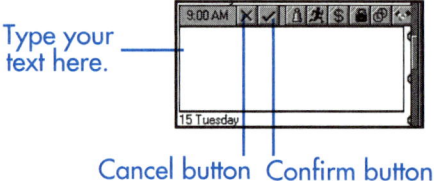

Type your text here.

Cancel button   Confirm button

Figure 6.1   The appointment window.

7. Type in the text for your appointment.

8. Click on the Confirm button to schedule the appointment.

Cancel That!   If you made a mistake or chose the wrong time slot, you can get out of the appointment window by clicking on the Cancel button or by pressing Esc.

The appointment window disappears when you click on the Confirm button, and the appointment text appears on the Calendar page. If you have too many appointments to be displayed in a single day's view, you can click on the down-arrow icon at the bottom of the day text area to see more appointments. You can also change to a view that gives more space to each day.

Editing Text in an Appointment

You can change appointment text at any time. You might, for example, want to change text about a meeting to compare the number of people who actually attended to those

Scheduling Appointments with the Calendar 29

who accepted invitations. You also might reschedule an appointment, opting to leave the original appointment in place with an explanation for why you rescheduled.

Here's how you edit existing text in an appointment:

1. Click on the Calendar tab to activate the Calendar.

2. Navigate to the appointment that needs editing.

3. Place the insertion point into the text by clicking on the text.

4. Edit the text.

5. Click on the Confirm button (it's identified by a green check mark) to save your changes.

The appointment window disappears when you click on the Confirm button, just as it did when you first made this appointment. The edited appointment text now appears on the Calendar page.

Changing the Day of an Appointment

If your appointments need rescheduling, Calendar makes the job easy and fast. You can use the drag-and-drop method to make rescheduling a snap!

Moving Violations You can only drag-and-drop an appointment to another day if you can see both days of the calendar while doing it. You might have to change the view in order to see both days.

Here's how you move an appointment from one day to the next:

1. Navigate to the appointment. Make sure you can see both the old and the new appointment days at the same time.

2. Place the pointer over the appointment to be moved.

3. Drag-and-drop the appointment onto another day on the Calendar. Figure 6.2 shows you the clock icon that replaces the pointer arrow when you drag-and-drop an appointment.

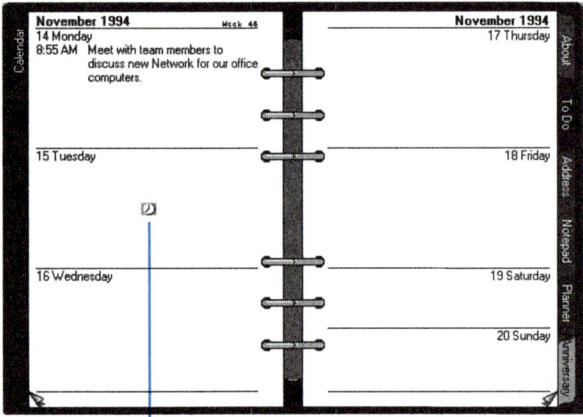

The Clock icon replaces the arrow pointer when dragging an appointment.

Figure 6.2 Using drag-and-drop to move an appointment.

Deleting an Appointment

Sooner or later, one of your appointments will be cancelled and will not be rescheduled. With Calendar, it's easy to dispose of those pesky cancellations. All you have to do is drag-and-drop the defunct appointment into the trash. The Trash icon is both located and explained in Figure 6.3 (with a little help from Organizer's Bubble help utility).

Scheduling Appointments with the Calendar   31

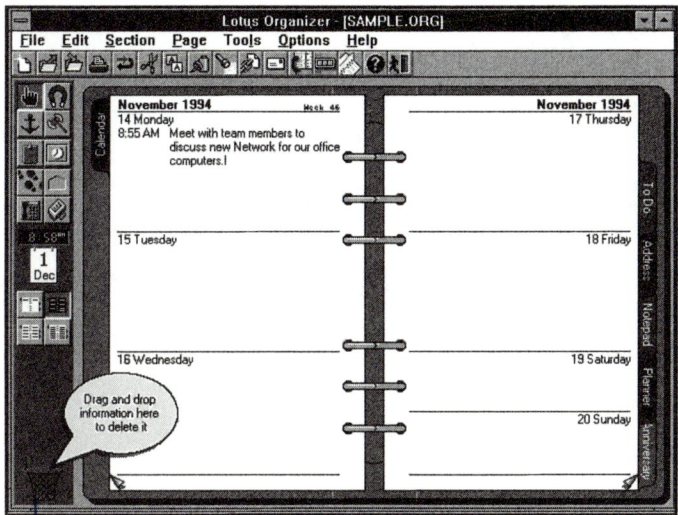

Trash icon

Figure 6.3 The Trash.

Whoops! You can retrieve a deleted appointment from the Trash by selecting **U**ndo from the **E**dit menu. (You can also click on the Undo SmartIcon. Act quickly, though; you can only save the last text trashed!

In this lesson, you learned how to make and manage appointments. In the next lesson, you'll learn how to use the Calendar to set alarms, launch programs at specific times, and associate costs with appointments.

Lesson 7

Using the TimeTracker to Adjust Appointments

In this lesson, you'll learn how to use the TimeTracker to change the length and time of an appointment.

What Is the TimeTracker?

By default, the Calendar makes appointments for you that last 60 minutes. However, sometimes an hour isn't the right amount of time for the appointment. You might need to make more than one appointment in an hour. Or you might need to allocate more than one hour for a weekly staff meeting or a seminar.

You can change the length and time of the appointment with the *TimeTracker*. The TimeTracker is a graphic representation of the time allotted to an appointment. It is basically displayed as two clocks that show the starting and ending times for the appointment. The duration of the appointment is shown in a small box between the two clocks. You can drag the elements of the TimeTracker either up or down to adjust your appointment.

In Figure 7.1, you'll see that a vertical green bar is displayed to the left of the clocks. That bar represents the duration of the current appointment, which means that its length is relative to the length of the appointment. If you've already made other appointments for that day, they will be represented by red bars.

Using the TimeTracker to Adjust Appointments   33

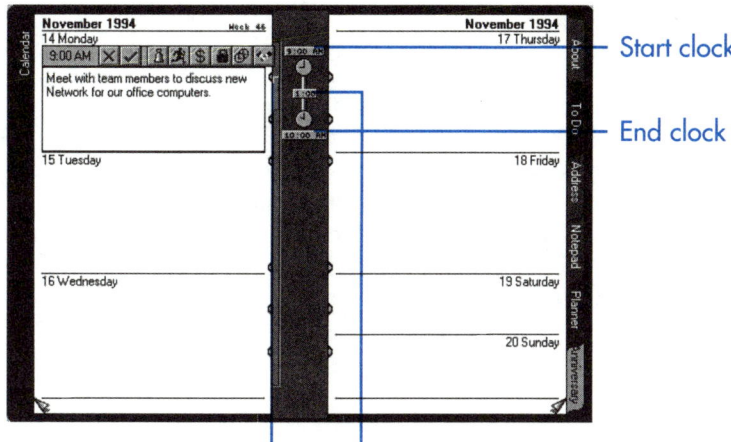

Figure 7.1 Focus on the TimeTracker.

Changing the Length of an Appointment

By default, the Calendar only lets you choose time slots that start on the hour or at half past the hour. However, you might have an appointment at 9:45 or 3:15. If that's the case, you can change the starting time with the TimeTracker. It automatically adjusts starting and ending times by five-minute increments. Here's how:

1. Open the Organizer file that contains your Calendar.

2. Click on the Calendar section tab.

3. Navigate to the appropriate appointment.

4. Click on the appointment text to open the appointment window and the TimeTracker.

5. Drag the upper clock to change the beginning time or the lower clock to change the ending time for the appointment. The duration time will change as you drag the clocks up and down.

6. Click on the Confirm button to save your changes.

> **Standard Deviation** If you want to change the duration for *all* appointments, you can set the default duration time to a new number. For example, you can set the default to 30 minutes so your appointments are automatically scheduled to last a half hour. See Lesson 9 for more details on changing Calendar defaults.

Changing the Time of an Appointment

If an appointment is rescheduled, you can move it to the new time with the TimeTracker. To change the time of an appointment:

1. Navigate to the appointment.

2. Click on the appointment text to open the appointment window and the TimeTracker.

3. Drag the duration time (*not* the clocks) either up or down. The display will change to reflect the new appointment time as you move it.

4. Click on the Confirm button to save your changes.

> **Speedy Switch** If you want to move an appointment in 30-minute increments instead of 5-minute increments, hold down the Shift key as you drag the duration time displayed in the middle of the TimeTracker.

When moving an appointment to a new time, look at the vertical red bars to see when you have other appointments scheduled. The TimeTracker won't let you drag the current appointment into a time slot that is already occupied.

Using the TimeTracker to Adjust Appointments

If you accidentally try to schedule conflicting appointments, the green bar that represents the current appointment will jump to the next available time slot.

The Disappearing Duration Time If you set the duration of your appointment to less than 60 minutes, you might not see the duration time displayed.

In this lesson, you learned how to use the TimeTracker to adjust appointments. In the next lesson, you'll learn how to set alarms, launch applications at specified times, and associate costs to appointments.

Lesson 8

Adding Extras to Your Appointments

In this lesson, you'll learn how to set alarms, launch an application at a preset time, and associate costs to appointments.

Using the Options in the Appointment Window

There are several "extras" you should consider while scheduling appointments. For example, do you need to set an alarm to remind yourself that there are ten minutes until an important meeting? Should you associate a cost with an appointment? Organizer lets you do these things and more.

Setting Alarms

Calendar helps you remember important appointments by letting you set alarms. You can specify whether you want the alarm to be just a dialog box, or if you want it to play a sound as well. You can set the alarm to go off up to four hours before an appointment.

Here's how you can set alarms for your appointments:

1. Open the appropriate appointment window.

2. Click on the Alarm button, shown in Figure 8.1. (It's marked with a bell icon.) The Alarm dialog box will open.

Adding Extras to Your Appointments   37

Alarm button

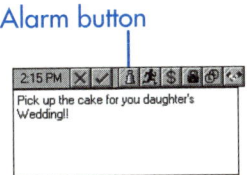

Figure 8.1   The appointment window and the Alarm button.

Wired for Sound   Organizer uses the PC's speaker to make sounds. Make sure your computer's speaker is plugged in if you want to take advantage of Organizer's sound capability.

3. Using the Alarm dialog box, shown in Figure 8.2, decide which tune you want to use:

- Click on the down-arrow button, and use the vertical scroll bar to review the tunes available. Click on a tune to select it for playing.

- If you want to preview a jingle, click on the Sample tune check box, and then click on the tune you want to hear.

- If you don't want to hear any music when the alarm goes off, deselect the Tune check box.

Select the **T**une check box if you want the alarm to be musical.   Click on the down arrow button to reveal the list of tunes.

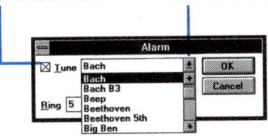

Figure 8.2   The Alarm dialog box.

4. Enter the number of minutes that you wish the alarm to go off in advance of the appointment in the **Ring . . . minutes before** text box. You can choose any number up to 240.

5. Click on the OK button to close the Alarm dialog box, and save your changes.

When your alarm goes off, you'll see a dialog box posted on your screen. This alarm dialog box will be displayed in the foreground while you're using any Windows application. If you've enabled the playing of tunes, you'll hear the tune you chose and see a dialog box with your appointment text displayed inside it. Note that Organizer must be running in order for your alarms to go off at all.

Running Applications at a Preset Time

Organizer's Calendar can run applications while you're away from your desk. You can start an application and a related document file, if you want. In short, Calendar will run any command line that is normally okay to run from Program Manager's Run dialog box.

Here's how you run a program using Calendar:

1. Open the appointment window for the day and time that you want your program launched.

2. Click on the Run Program button, shown in Figure 8.3. (It's the one that looks like a running person.)

3. In the Run Program dialog box, shown in Figure 8.4, type the path and file name of the program you want to run in the **R**un text box. If you don't remember the exact path and file name, browse for it by clicking on the Browse button.

Adding Extras to Your Appointments   39

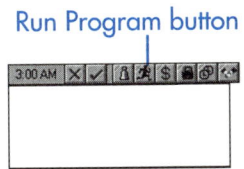

Figure 8.3 The appointment window and the Run Program button.

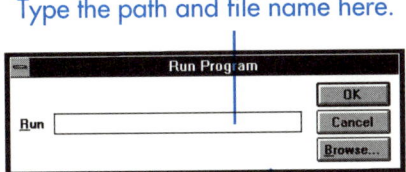

Figure 8.4 The Run Program dialog box.

4. Click on the OK button to close the Run Program dialog box.

You'll notice that there is a little triangle at the top-left of the Run Program icon to indicate that it is activated. If you click on the button again it will be deactivated, and the program will not be launched.

Didn't Work? Remember, Organizer has to be running (either minimized or full-screen) at the time the application is supposed to be launched.

Associating Costs to Appointments

If you're one of the folks who have to track their time against projects, budgets, cost center codes, or customer purchase order numbers, you'll be interested in learning how to use Organizer's Calendar to attribute and track costs against appointments.

Here's how you assign a cost to an appointment:

1. Open the appropriate appointment window.

2. Click on the Cost Codes button, shown in Figure 8.5. (It's labeled with a dollar sign.)

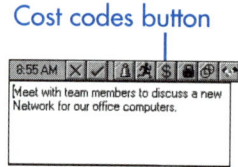

Figure 8.5 The appointment window and the Cost Codes button.

3. In the Cost Codes dialog box, shown in Figure 8.6, enter the Customer code into the Customer Code text box. The Customer code can be as simple as the Customer's name (like a company name) or as systematic as a cost center number (probably provided by your company's Accounting department).

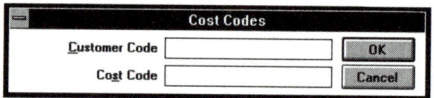

Figure 8.6 The Cost Codes dialog box.

4. Enter the amount you charge per hour for your time in the Cost Code text box.

5. Click on the OK button when you're finished.

Once you've set a cost code, a small indicator will be shown at the top-left corner of the Cost Codes button. You can turn off Cost Code tracking by clicking on the Cost

Codes button again. If you've disabled Cost Code tracking for an appointment, you can reinstate Cost Code tracking by again clicking once on the Cost Codes button.

In this lesson, you learned how to use Organizer's Calendar to set alarms, launch programs, and associate costs to appointments. In the next lesson, you'll learn how to set some of Calendar's preferences.

Lesson

Setting Calendar Preferences

In this lesson, you'll learn how to customize your Calendar.

Customizing Your Calendar

You can personalize your Calendar by changing its settings. For example, you can set your favorite duration of time for appointments as the default (discussed in Lesson 7). You can include or exclude weekends in your Calendar. You can decide how your Calendar pages are viewed by default, so you don't have to click on a view icon whenever you open your Calendar. You can even change the number of appointments that can be made every hour.

Here's how you customize Calendar options:

1. Open the Organizer file that contains your Calendar.

2. Click on the Calendar section tab.

3. Choose Calendar from the Options menu. The Calendar Options dialog box will open, like the one shown in Figure 9.1.

Setting Calendar Preferences 43

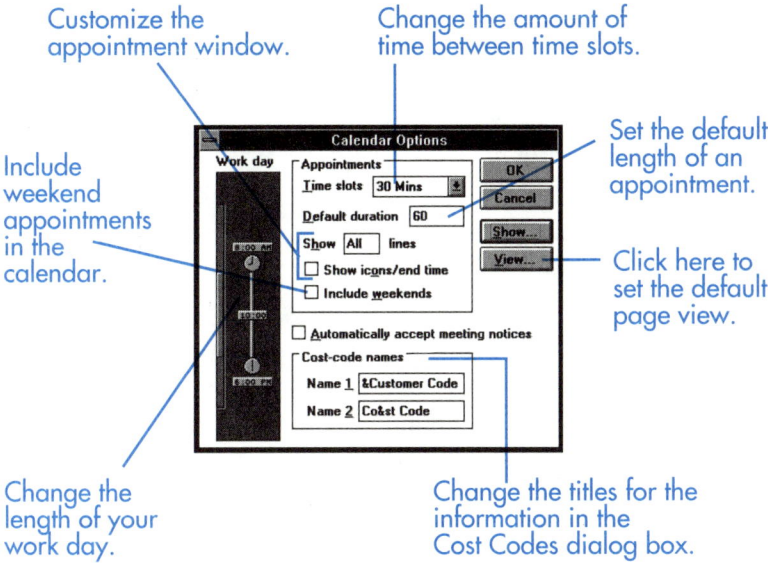

Figure 9.1 The Calendar Options dialog box.

4. Customize your Calendar by changing any of the following options:

- Change the length of your work day by dragging the clock elements of the Work day either up or down. The upper clock displays the day's start time, the lower clock denotes the end of the work day, and the middle display shows you the length of the day.

- Choose the points where time slots begin in each hour.

- Change the default duration if you want appointments to run shorter or longer by default.

- Determine how many lines can be displayed in a Calendar appointment.

- Toggle the display of icons that denote the use of additional Calendar features (like alarms and cost codes).

- Click on the Include weekends check box to include weekend appointments in your Calendar.

- If you want to keep track of something else besides "Customer Code" in the Cost Code dialog box, change the text in the Name 1 text box to suit your needs. Whatever you type into the Name 1 text box will appear in place of the words "Customer Code" when you open the Cost Code dialog box in the future. You can change the words "Cost Code" the same way.

- Click on the View button to customize the default page view when using the Calendar.

To Change or Not to Change If you aren't sure whether to change an option, or if you aren't sure what to change it to, you should probably leave it alone. After you've become more comfortable with the Calendar and developed your own style, you can open the Calendar Options dialog box again to change your preferences.

Displaying Information from Other Sections

The Calendar will display entries from other sections if you want it to. If you set up your Calendar to show the entries you made in the Anniversary section, you can remind yourself of an anniversary while you're scheduling an appointment. For example, say you are scheduling an appointment for next Tuesday. When you open the Calendar to Tuesday's date, you see a reminder that Tuesday is your wedding anniversary. (For more information on the Anniversary section, see Lesson 17.)

Here's how you customize Calendar to see information from other sections:

1. Open your Calendar by clicking on the Calendar section tab.

2. Choose Calendar from the Options menu.

3. Click on the Show button. The Calendar Options (Show) dialog box, shown in Figure 9.2, will open.

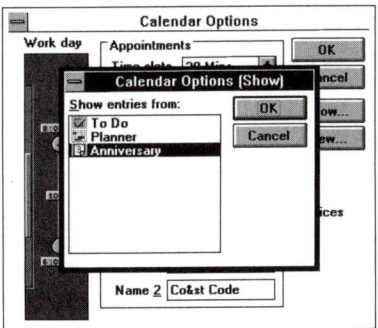

Figure 9.2 The Calendar Options (Show) dialog box.

Lesson 9

4. Select any of the items displayed in the Show entries from: list box to cause same-day commitments from those sections to be displayed in your Calendar—along with your Calendar appointments.

5. Click on the OK button to close the Calendar Options (Show) dialog box, and then click on the OK button to close the Calendar Options dialog box.

Now, you'll see entries from other sections in your Calendar. Calendar will display entries from other sections in a different color from your appointment text so it's easy to distinguish.

In this lesson, you learned about customizing your Calendar. In the next lesson, you'll learn about the To Do list, and how to keep your tasks organized more efficiently.

Lesson 10

Working with the To Do List

In this lesson, you'll learn about adding, removing, and managing tasks in Organizer's To Do list.

What Is the To Do List?

Organizer's To Do list is a single-page list that's made to accept any number of tasks. You can use the To Do list to plan and track almost every task you embark upon, and you can feed the information directly into your Calendar section without having to re-enter the same text there. When you've completed a task, you can mark it as "done." (A completed task has a line through it to denote its completion.) The To Do list even sorts its listing of tasks by priority.

The trick to managing an effective To Do list is to make sure you give yourself enough time to enter tasks and maintain their status. The sections in this lesson teach you how to do just that: add, remove, and manage items on your To Do list. For the sake of this lesson and of learning to use Organizer's To Do list, I'll be using the terms *task* and *item* interchangeably.

Adding Tasks to the To Do List

Most of us have more things to do in our lives that we can remember, let alone keep track of their priority and their current status. Organizer's To Do list allows you to enter as many items or tasks as you can find the time to enter.

Here's how you add a task to your To Do list:

1. Open an Organizer file.

2. Click on the To Do section tab on the right side of the Organizer's binder. The To Do list, shown in Figure 10.1, will open.

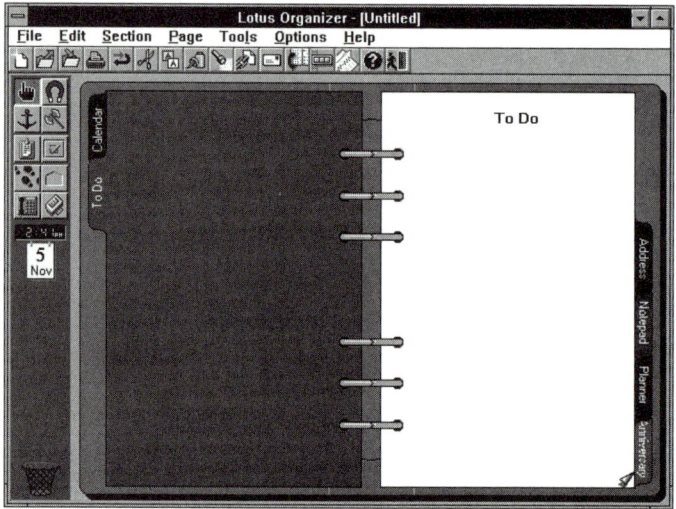

Figure 10.1 An empty To Do list.

3. Click anywhere on the To Do page to open the To Do dialog box (as shown in Figure 10.2).

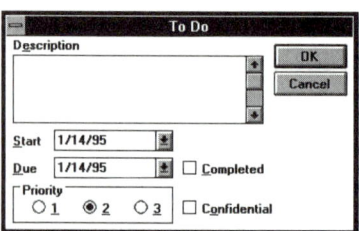

Figure 10.2 The To Do dialog box.

Working with the To Do List 49

4. Type the name of the task in the Description text box.

5. If the task isn't to be done today, select another date. Click on the Start down-arrow button to open the current month's calendar display. If you want, select another month by clicking on the left or right arrows, and then select a day of that month. Figure 10.3 shows you this Month display and the arrows used to switch between months.

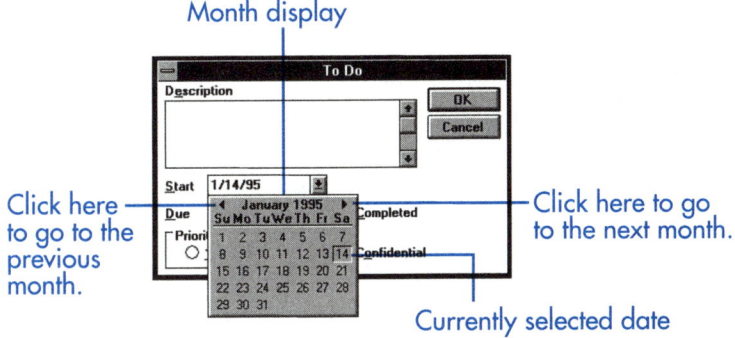

Figure 10.3 The Month display in the To Do dialog box.

6. Select a Due date the same way you selected a Start date.

7. Under Priority, click on one of three option buttons. The To Do list will sort a day's tasks by the priority number you assign.

8. If you consider the new task to be confidential, click on the Confidential check box—otherwise, leave it blank. It you use a Password, other people will be limited by the security level you assigned.

9. Click on the OK button to close the To Do dialog box and place your new task on the To Do list.

Managing Items

Once you've added items to your To Do list, you'll be ready to manage them. You may want to change the date or the priority, and you'll surely want to mark them as being completed once they're done.

Here's how you manage your tasks on the To Do list:

1. Open the To Do section.

2. Click on any task to open the To Do dialog box.

3. Select any of these options:

    - If you've completed the selected task, check the Completed dialog box and the task will be crossed out on the To Do list. When you complete a task, the priority number doesn't change, it just goes to the bottom of the list. All completed tasks are sorted by date, and then priority.

    - If you want to assign the selected task to another date, click on the Start and Due down-arrow buttons to select other dates for your task.

    - If you want to change the order in which the selected task is slated to be completed, click on a different Priority option button.

4. Click on the OK button to close the To Do dialog box and view your changes on the To Do list.

In the example in Figure 10.4, I have completed the first of my tasks. That task has been moved to the bottom of the list until I decide to delete it altogether. I changed the priority of what used to be the second task on my list to Priority 1, just to make sure that it appeared before all of the other tasks for that same day.

Working with the To Do List 51

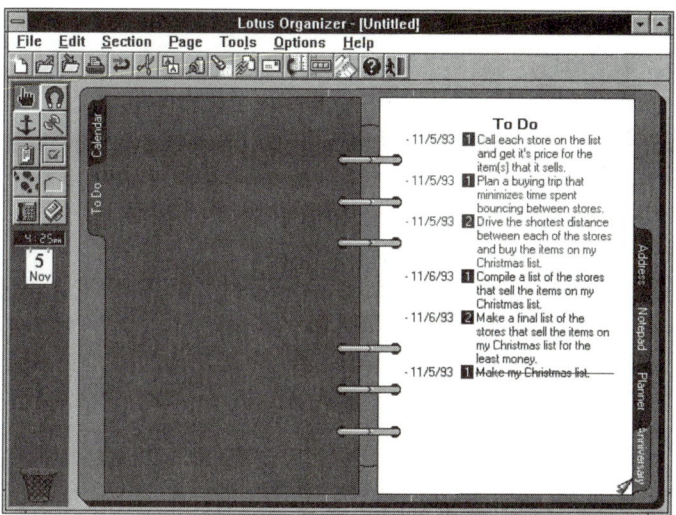

Figure 10.4 One item completed on my To Do list.

Telling Tasks Apart When your To Do list holds tasks to be done over a series of days, each day is differentiated by the color of its text. Tasks slated for day one will be green, day two will be blue, and so on. Tasks that have been completed will be displayed in black text with a red line through it.

Removing Items from the To Do List

Once you've completed a task, you can either let it stay at the bottom of your To Do list (noted as completed), or you can delete it altogether. It's entirely up to you. By default, Organizer's To Do list will not delete your completed tasks. You must do it yourself.

Here's how to remove tasks from your To Do list:

1. Open your To Do list.

2. Drag-and-drop the task into the Trash.

> **Deletion Anxiety** You can retrieve a deleted task by selecting Undo from the Edit menu, or by clicking on the Undo SmartIcon. Remember: the Trash holds only one task, so you can only retrieve the last task trashed!

In this lesson, you learned how to use the To Do list to create and manage tasks. In the next lesson, you'll learn how to use Organizer's Notepad section to help you organize your notes.

Lesson 11

Using the Notepad to Make a Note for Yourself

In this lesson, you'll learn how to use Organizer's Notepad to keep track of important text.

What Is the Notepad?

Organizer's Notepad is a computerized replacement for a pad of paper. You can note information that takes up more space than a single page. You can also place graphics into your notes, like charts and graphs. You can use the Notepad to document thoughts, methods, and even events.

Notepad considers all pages to be part of one single blank pad of paper. Notepad adds new pages as though it were adding a new chapter to a book that's blank (so far). Your Notepad will even build a table of contents for you as you add pages. Each page (or group of pages) will be indexed as a new entry, or *chapter*.

Making Notepad Pages

When you first create a Notepad page, you need to specify what kind of information it is expected to hold. Once you create your page, you can then fill it with information.

Lesson 11

Follow these steps to create a Notepad page:

1. Open an Organizer file.

2. Click on the Notepad section tab on the right side of the Organizer's binder. The Notepad will open to an empty Contents page, as shown in Figure 11.1.

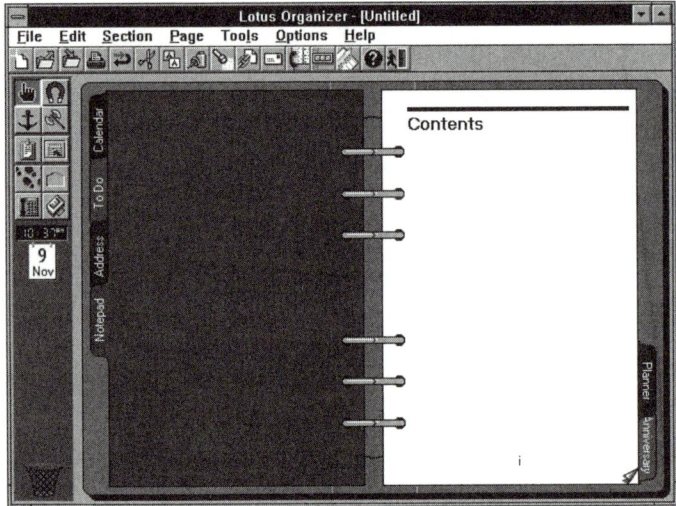

Figure 11.1 An empty Contents page in the Notepad.

3. Click on the Contents page, and the Notepad Page Insert dialog box will open, as shown in Figure 11.2. This is where you title and create a table of contents for your note.

Using the Notepad to Make a Note for Yourself 55

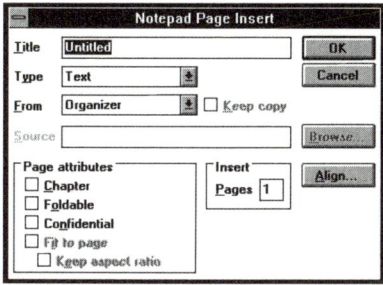

Figure 11.2 The Notepad Page Insert dialog box.

4. Enter the name of your note into the **Title** text box.

5. From the **Type** drop-down list, select a type of information for your Notepad page. Click on the down-arrow button to review a list of available selections. Click on one of these choices to select it:

   Blank A blank page is used as a spacer between other Notepad pages.

   Text Text is made up of characters that can be created using your keyboard. You can paste text onto a Text page, too.

   Metafile A Metafile is one kind of picture file format used by some Windows applications. Metafiles have a file name extension of WMF.

   Bitmap A bitmap is also one kind of a file that can hold a picture. Notepad will accept a bitmap file that has a file name extension of BMP. Windows Paintbrush creates bitmap (*.BMP) files.

   Links Links are connections to other applications. Choose this page type if you want this page to provide a list of current links.

6. In the From list box, select where your note will come from. If you're typing in the contents of the note, select Organizer. If the contents are to come from the Clipboard (*DDE*) or a file, select that instead.

> **Dynamic Data Exchange (DDE)** This feature of Windows 3.1 allows applications to communicate and actively pass information through the Clipboard. Instead of just pasting a regular copy of the information into your file, you are pasting a copy that is linked to the original file. As long as both programs are active, whenever you update the original, the copy is updated as well.

> **Name Your Source** If you select DDE or File, you'll be prompted to specify the source (the file name or DDE application). If you select DDE, Organizer will check the originating file and update your note with any changes found in the specified file (source). Select DDE if you're going to paste a spreadsheet or database file that's going to be updated.

7. Click on one of the Page attributes options to tell Notepad how to handle the pages.

8. Click on the Pages text box, and type the number of pages you'd like to use in this chapter.

9. Click on the OK button to create your Notepad page.

If you opted to create a text page, you'll see that Notepad added your new page to the existing Notepad and to the table of contents.

Using the Notepad to Make a Note for Yourself   57

Looking at a Notepad's Table of Contents

When you add pages to Notepad, your pages are represented on the table of contents by the title you chose for them. If you don't specify a title for the page(s) you add to your Notepad, "Untitled" will be used.

You can customize Notepad to show a shortened version of a table of contents or no table at all. Follow these steps to customize Notepad's display of your table of contents:

1. Open your Notepad.

2. Select Notepad from the Options menu. The Notepad Options dialog box will open, like the one in Figure 11.3.

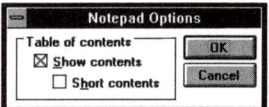

Figure 11.3   The Notepad Options dialog box.

3. If you want to see the table of contents when you open your Notepad, click on the Show contents check box. Figure 11.4 shows you what a sample table of contents looks like.

4. Click on the Short contents check box if you want to see the page-number level of detail omitted from the table of contents.

Lesson 11

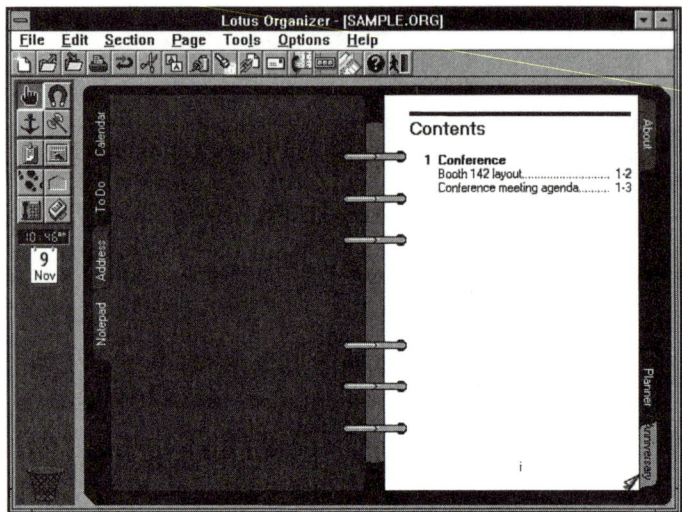

Figure 11.4 A sample table of contents.

Pasting into a Notepad Page

If you create a Notepad page that will accept bitmaps, you can paste a graphic picture onto a Notepad page from the Clipboard. First, of course, you'll have to create that page or change an existing page to one that will accept information from the Clipboard (specify this in the Notepad Page Edit dialog box). If you've already created a text page and you want to paste text onto it, that process is simple, too. Here's the only caveat: you can't paste graphics onto a text page, and you can't paste text onto a graphics page.

Here's how you paste information onto a Notepad page:

1. Go to the page in your Notepad that is to accept the text or graphics from the Clipboard.

Using the Notepad to Make a Note for Yourself 59

> **Quick Flip** You can use the Page Up and Page Down keys on your keyboard to flip through the pages of your Notepad, if you don't want to use the mouse to flip pages by clicking on the lower-outside corners.

2. Click on the page title to open the Notepad Page Edit dialog box. If you want to paste graphics onto a page, select Bitmap from the Type list and Clipboard from the From list, and then close the dialog box.

If you selected Bitmap from the Clipboard, you'll now see the contents of the Clipboard pasted onto the page. If you opted to paste text, paste Clipboard text into the text page. (Select the **Paste** command from the **Edit** menu, press Ctrl+V, or click on the Paste SmartIcon.) To save your work, just turn the page.

Deleting Notepad Pages

Deleting Notepad pages (or a series of pages) is the same as deleting anything in Organizer: you simply drag-and-drop them into the Trash. After you've thrown away the page(s), flames in the Trash will flare up, signifying that you've successfully trashed a page.

In this lesson, you learned how to work with Organizer's Notepad. In the next lesson, you'll learn how to plan events and schedule meetings using Organizer's Planner.

Lesson 12

Working with the Planner

In this lesson, you'll learn how to change your view of the Planner, add events, use the Calendar in conjunction with the Planner, and work with resources, such as meeting rooms.

What Is the Planner?

Organizer's Planner is intended to resemble a fold-out chart that you can continuously update. (It's shown in Figure 12.1) You use the Planner to allocate blocks of time to events. Each year (through 2000) is represented by its own chart in the Planner. When you open the Planner, the current year's chart is displayed as a folded page. To see the entire chart, you unfold the page the same way you'd have to unfold it to see a year's events if the Planner were a hard-copy tool sitting in front of you on your desk.

Planner's charts show you colored blocks that represent planned events over the course of the year. Months are listed from top-to-bottom. The days in each month are displayed along the top of the chart from left to right. Since months vary in the number of Sundays (for example), you may see a month's schedule begin on the second or even the third day of the week.

Working with the Planner

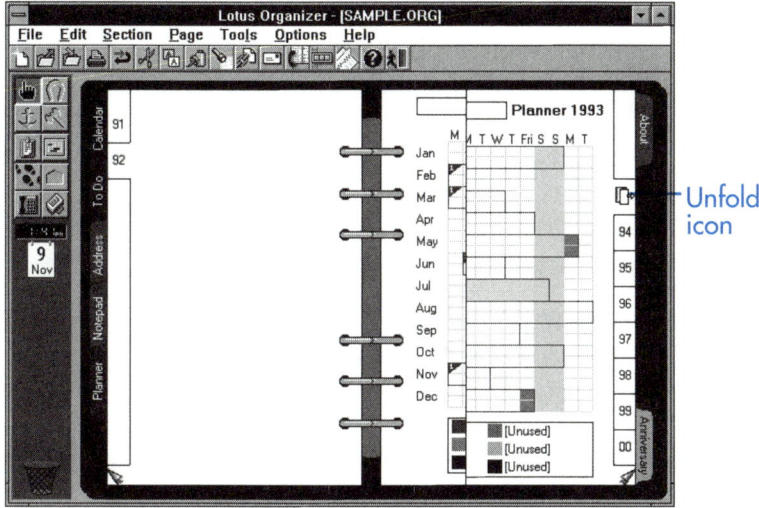

Figure 12.1 The folded-up Planner section.

The beginning of a month is marked with a red icon displaying the number "1." The chart divides each day into AM and PM. Weekends are grayed-out by default, but you can include weekends in your plans if you change Planner's settings.

In this lesson, I'm going to use my Planner to organize events in the mythical life of an Advertising Executive. You can find the same chart shown in this book in your \ORGANIZE\SAMPLE directory. The file is called SAMPLE.ORG. (This sample Organizer file was installed during the Organizer Setup process.) You can use this SAMPLE.ORG file to experiment with Planner and go through the steps in this lesson on-line if you want.

Changing Your View of the Planner

You have to be able to see an entire chart before you can schedule any events. In order to see an entire year, you need to unfold Planner's charts. (See Figure 12.2.) To open Planner's charts to view entire years, follow these steps:

1. Open an Organizer file. (If you want to follow along with my example, use \ORGANIZE\SAMPLE\SAMPLE.ORG.)

2. Click on the Planner section tab. The Planner will open to the current year.

3. Click on the Unfold icon. It's located along the right edge of the chart. (It looks like a folded page with an arrow on it.) The Planner will open up.

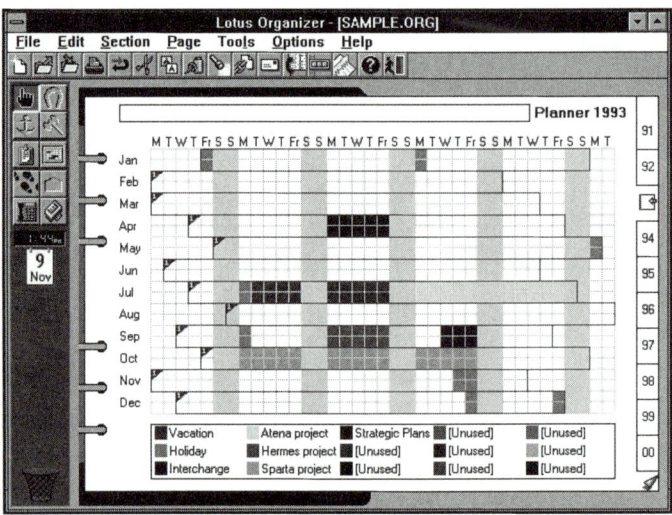

Figure 12.2 Planner's unfolded view of SAMPLE.ORG.

Note that the date, time (either AM or PM), and event name are displayed in the text box that runs along the top of each chart. Move the mouse over the chart to see this information change to reflect the position of the mouse on the chart. To select another year, click on one of the year logos displayed along the right border of the Planner.

Working with the Planner 63

Adding Events

Even though there are at least two ways to place a planned event on your chart, we'll focus on the Planner's unique method because it's the simplest and fastest way to go. It's a little like the drag-and-drop methods described in previous lessons, except that you don't have to hold down the mouse button to drag the block and drop it.

Follow these steps to add an event to your Planner:

1. With the Planner unfolded, click once (*don't* hold down the mouse button) on any colored block in the legend at the base of the chart. The mouse pointer will now look like the colored block you selected.

2. Move the mouse across the chart to an available, open date.

3. When the block is positioned exactly where you want it, click your mouse button once to place it on your chart.

4. If you want to change the name of a color block, click on the text next to that colored block, and type the new name.

> **Recurring Events** If you want to schedule multiple days with one block, hold down the Shift key when you select that block, and then hold down the mouse button while you paint in the desired time slots. Release the mouse button when you're done painting.

> **Presto Chango** If you drag the block to a time slot that's already allocated to an event, your newly-dragged block will disappear when you drop it.

Lesson 12

Using the Planner with the Calendar

Conceivably, you could double-book yourself if you make a Calendar appointment and a planned event for the same day. To help prevent this, Organizer allows you to view appointment commitments from the Calendar section in Planner's chart format.

Here's how you can display Calendar information in a Planner-style chart:

1. With a Planner chart unfolded, select Planner from the Options menu. The Planner Options dialog box will open, as shown in Figure 12.3.

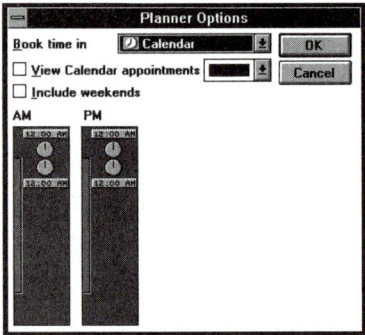

Figure 12.3 The Planner Options dialog box.

2. Select Calendar from the items displayed in the Book time in list box.

3. Click on the View Calendar appointments check box.

4. Click on the down-arrow button to view the list of available colors used for displaying Calendar appointment text in Planner charts.

Working with the Planner

5. Click on the OK button to close the Planner Options dialog box and see Calendar appointments displayed on a Planner chart.

Calendar appointments are displayed on a Planner chart as colored lines rather than colored blocks. Note that you can't view both Calendar appointments and Planner events on one chart.

> **Quid Pro Quo** To return to viewing Planner events, re-open the Planner Options dialog box, and select Planner instead of Calendar.

In this lesson, you learned how to use the Planner. In the next lesson, you'll learn how to set up your Address section.

Lesson 13

Setting Up the Address Section

In this lesson, you'll learn how to set up the Address section, change address views, and add, change, and delete addresses.

Using the Address Section

Organizer's Address section is an electronic address book. It can keep track of as many addresses as you want. To enter an address, you use a blank template (it appears as the first page when you open the Address section). Looking at your entered addresses is as easy as turning the pages!

All of the bits of information about a single person are kept in their own respective *fields*, based on what kind of information it is. All of the fields for one address are organized into a single *record* for that person. All records are organized into a *database*: your Address section.

> **Fields** A dedicated space in a database record. Specific types of information are stored in specific fields. For example, you store an address in a field used only for that type of information. Each record in a database holds fields that are found in every record.

Setting Up the Address Section   67

Database A file or a group of related files that are designed to hold information. A database is basically a list, with many columns of information.

Changing Address Views

Organizer lets you view the Address section in one of four views. The views display your addresses in different page layouts. That's why each view is named after the page layout used for each.

Here's how you change your view of the Address section:

1. Open an Organizer file.

2. Click on the Address section tab to open it. The Address section will appear, like the one shown in Figure 13.1. The first page is a blank record template, waiting to be filled out.

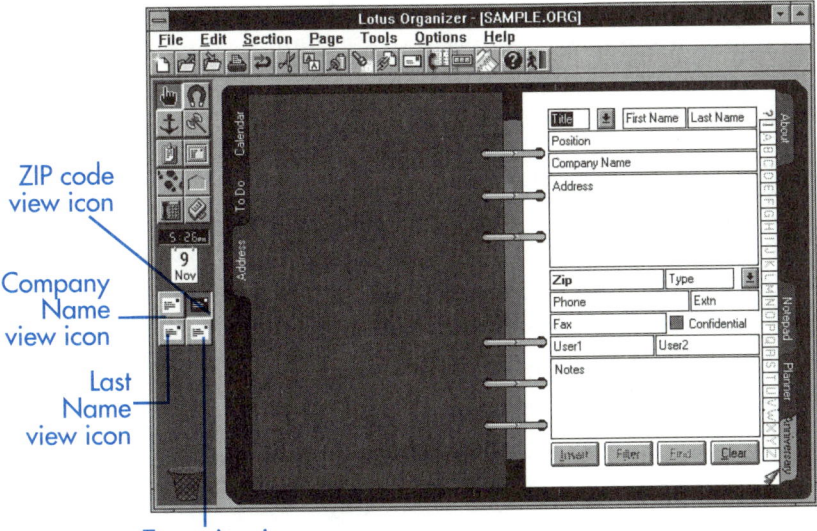

ZIP code view icon

Company Name view icon

Last Name view icon

Type view icon

Figure 13.1 The Address section.

3. Click on any of the four view icons (located at the left side of Organizer's screen) to change the view.

> **Sorting Your Entries** Your entries in the Address section are in a certain order, sorted by a certain field. With each view, the field that the section is sorted by changes. In Figure 13.1, you'll note that the ZIP field is in bold text. When you see a field name in bold text, that means that the current view is sorting all address records by the contents of that field.

If you want, click on each of the view icons to see the different views. Notice that the page layout of the template doesn't vary when you change views. The only thing that changes is the order in which the addresses are sorted.

It's useful to change views if you're searching for a record when you have limited information at hand. For example, if you only know a person's last name (but you'd recognize the record if you saw the rest of the info), you can find that record by skimming the database. To do that, click on the Last Name view icon, and then skim the database until you find that last name and the person's address record. Check out Lesson 14 for more on finding text in the Address section.

Adding an Address

Adding an address to Organizer's Address section is easy. You simply open the Organizer file, go to the Address section, and enter the address into a new, empty template.

Follow these instructions to add addresses to the Address section:

1. Open the Address section.

Setting Up the Address Section 69

2. When you begin adding a new Address record, the highlight will be in the Title field. Click on the down-arrow button to view the selections available, and then click on one to choose it.

3. Press the Tab key to move the highlight into the next field. Begin typing to over-write the highlighted field label.

Keep repeating step 3 until you've entered all of the information into this person's record. Don't forget that the down-arrow buttons reveal lists from which you can select words commonly used in those fields.

> **Back Up!** You can move backward through a record by pressing Shift+Tab.

Changing an Address

Addresses often need to be updated. When people move or change jobs, their addresses and phone numbers change. You can edit any address that needs updating. Here's how:

1. Go to the address you want to change by clicking on the Address section tab and then using the Page Up or Page Down keys.

2. Click on the part of the address you want to change, placing the insertion point into that field, and then make your changes.

> **Automatic Save** As soon as you make changes, Organizer updates your file on disk.

Deleting an Address

When people move, get married, or pass away, it sometimes makes sense to delete their addresses from your Address section. You can delete unused or unwanted addresses from the Address section by following these steps:

1. Open the Address section.

2. Navigate to the address you want to delete.

3. Drag-and-drop the defunct address into the Trash.

> **Oops!** If you delete an address and suddenly realize that you've made a dreadful mistake, you can undelete it by selecting Undo from the Edit menu. You can also click on the Undo SmartIcon. Don't forget to Undo the deletion before you continue—you can only retrieve the last item you threw away!

In this lesson, you learned how to set up your Address section. In the next lesson, you'll learn more about working with the information in your Address section.

Lesson 14

Working with the Address Section

In this lesson, you'll learn how to find addresses and change the sort order of addresses.

Finding an Address

If your Address section is bulging at the seams, it's probably getting harder and harder to find an address. Here's how you can quickly find addresses in your Address section:

1. Open the Organizer file that contains your addresses.

2. Select Search from the Edit menu, or press F3. The Search dialog box will open.

> **Search and Seizure** To quickly open the Search dialog box, click on the Search SmartIcon. It looks like a flashlight.

3. Type the information you want to search for into the For text box.

4. Click on Address in the In list box. Now you're ready to search. In Figure 14.1, I'm telling Organizer to search for the word *Jennifer* in the Address section.

Lesson 14

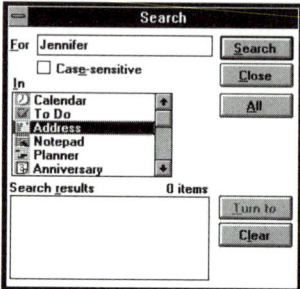

Figure 14.1 The Search dialog box.

5. Click on the Search button.

6. Double-click on the address you're looking for in the Search results list box (there may be more than one entry listed).

7. Click on the Close button to clear the Search dialog box from the screen.

The Address section should now be opened to the address you seek. If you're not looking at the right address, open the Search dialog box again, and search for text you know is in the record. You can Search for text in any address record as many times as you like.

Changing the Sort Order

Organizer's Address section allows you to review your addresses in one of four sort-orders: Company Name, Zip code, Last Name, and Type.

For example, you may have many people from a single company listed in your Address section. You can change the view so that the Address section is sorted by Company Name, so that you can view the addresses of people who work for the same company one-after-another.

Here's how you sort your addresses in any of the four ways available:

Working with the Address Section

1. Open the Address section.

2. Select Address from the Options menu. The Address Options dialog box, like the one shown in Figure 14.2, will open. (In this figure, I opted to sort by Company.)

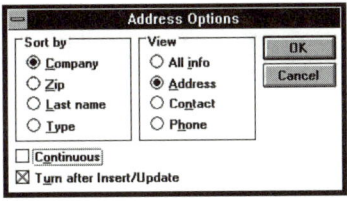

Figure 14.2 The Address Options dialog box.

3. In the Sort by group box, click on the option button that's next to the sort you want to use.

4. Click on the OK button to close the Address Options dialog box and see your new sort order reflected in your Address section.

In this lesson, you learned how to work with your Address section. In the next lesson, you'll learn how to import and export address information.

Lesson 15

Importing and Exporting Addresses

In this lesson, you'll learn about importing information from other sources. You'll also learn about exporting addresses to other file formats.

Importing Addresses

Personal Information Managers, database programs, and even word processors can be used to keep lists of addresses. You can copy those addresses into Organizer's Address section. Organizer will accept addresses found in dBASE III/IV, Windows Cardfile, and ASCII text files (Windows Notepad's format). Of course, you can also import other Organizer Address listings into your own files.

> **Test Drive** I suggest that you try the importing process with the sample files located in \ORGANIZE\SAMPLE instead of your own Organizer file. When you're comfortable with the process, then go ahead and use your own Organizer file. I'm going to use sample files from that subdirectory to illustrate examples.

Importing and Exporting Addresses 75

Apples-to-Apples The addresses stored in some ASCII text files will need to be *set up* before you can import them. Each field of info needs to be enclosed in quotes. Each field needs to be separated from other fields with commas. All fields in one record need to be on the same line. Each record needs to end in a carriage return (the editor you use may not actually display a carriage return symbol).

Here's how you import address lists created by other applications:

1. Open your Organizer file.

2. Click on the Address section tab.

3. Select Import from the File menu. The Import dialog box will open, as shown in Figure 15.1.

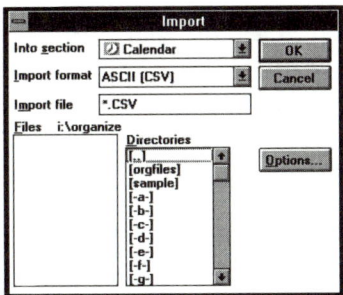

Figure 15.1 The Import dialog box.

4. Select Address from the Into section list box.

5. Select the type of file that you're importing from the Import format list box, for example, .CSV.

6. Use the **Directories** list box to select the directory where the imported file resides.

Lesson 15

Field Mapping Whenever you copy database information from one file into another file, you have to decide where you want each type of information to reside in the recipient file.

You're Still in Kansas . . . If you're a spreadsheet user, it might help you to think of database fields as spreadsheet column or row labels.

FYI As you learned in an earlier lesson, databases (like Organizer's Address section) keep information in fields. You have to match up the fields in the imported database with fields in your Address database.

7. Double-click on the file that's to be imported (for example, ADDRESS.CSV). The Field Mapping dialog box will open, as shown in Figure 15.2.

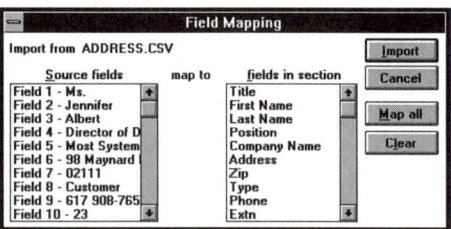

Figure 15.2 The Field Mapping dialog box.

8. Use the dialog box to tell Organizer where you want to place the imported information into your Address database.

9. Click on the top-left field listed in the **S**ource fields list box. In our example, it's **FIELD 1 - Ms.**.

Importing and Exporting Addresses 77

Save Time! If you're importing another Organizer address, you can just click on the **Map all** button and skip steps 9–12.

10. Click on the Title field in the fields in section list box. See the line that connected these two fields? These two fields are now mapped.

11. Repeat step 10 until all of the fields in both lists are mapped.

12. Click on the Import button to import the data in the import file into the Address section's database.

You'll see a progress bar during the import process. Organizer will tell you which records can't be imported (usually because of formatting problems) and how many records were successfully imported.

Duplicating Work! If the same record exists in both the imported file and Address section database section prior to importing, you'll end up with duplicate records in your Address database after importing.

Exporting Addresses

A database or word processing application can access the addresses in your Organizer's Address database. You need to export the records in your Address section into another file format supported by Organizer. Organizer will copy your Address records into a file that can be used by dBASE III/IV or any word processor that can read an ASCII text file.

When Organizer exports information, it organizes it so that these other applications can accept and utilize it. This process is called *Field Mapping*. See the "Importing Addresses" section in this lesson for more on Field Mapping.

Here's how you export addresses from Organizer's Address section:

1. Open the Address section.

2. Select Export from the File menu. The Export dialog box will open, shown in Figure 15.3.

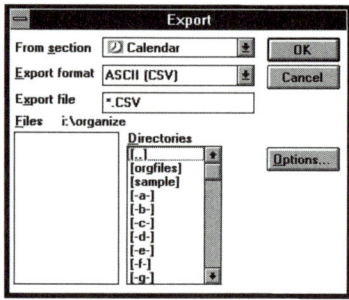

Figure 15.3 The Export dialog box.

3. Select Address from the From section list box.

4. Select the type of file that you're importing from the Export format list box.

5. Type the name of the file that will hold your exported records into the Export file text box.

6. Use the Directories list box to select the directory where the exported file is to reside.

7. Click on the OK button. The Field Mapping dialog box opens. You'll use this dialog box to tell Organizer where you want to place the imported information into your exported file.

8. Click on the top-left field listed in the fields in section list box.

Logging and Tracking Phone Calls 81

Phone icon

Figure 16.1 The Phone icon in Organizer's toolbox.

Autodial Shortcut While using the Address section, you can Autodial someone listed by navigating to the address and then dragging-and-dropping it onto the Phone icon in the Toolbox.

3. The Dial dialog box will open, as shown in Figure 16.2. Begin typing the number you want to dial.

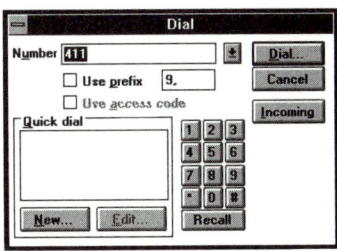

Figure 16.2 The Dial dialog box.

Lesson 16

4. Click on the Use prefix check box if you need to use a code to gain access to an outside line, outbound watts line, or any other service your company's phone system offers.

> **You're the Boss!** You can apply the Use prefix feature to disable any dialing options enabled by your phone company, such as disabling call-waiting.

5. Click on the New button to add this number to your Quick dial list box. Type in the name of the person you're calling, when prompted, and select OK. That person's name and number will soon be showing in the Quick dial list box.

6. Click on the Dial button to cause your modem to dial the number shown in the Number text box. Your modem will now dial the phone for you.

7. When the Dial dialog box opens, click on the button that best describes the outcome of your call to place this call in your phone log.

8. If your call is answered, you can type notes into the Notes text box in the Call Log dialog box.

9. Click on the Hang up button when you're finished making your call so that the modem knows it's time to hang up.

> **A Hang Up** Some modems have a hard time hanging-up when you ask them to. If your modem fails to hang-up properly when you click on the Hang up button, click on the Phone icon again, but

Logging and Tracking Phone Calls

this time type **++ATH** instead of a phone number. Dialing this character sequence forces most Hayes-compatible modems to hang up. If the modem still doesn't hang up, click on the Retry button until you regain your dial tone.

The End When you click on the Hang up button, the Call Log dialog box closes. Make sure you type in all of your notes before you click on the Hang up button.

The **Q**uick dial list box will (in the future) display all calls made in this manner. If you just made a call, you should have one phone call logged.

Tracking Phone Calls

Tracking frequent calls is also a great way to find a phone number if you remember the content of the call but don't remember the name of the caller. Once you've logged calls, you can review your phone log to find a frequently dialed phone number, or the notes you kept while making a call.

Here's how you track logged phone calls:

1. Click on the Phone Log SmartIcon, shown in Figure 16.3.

2. The Phone Log dialog box will open. The first time you open your Phone Log, it may be empty. I made a few calls and committed them to the Phone Log so you could see what a working Phone Log looks like. It's shown in Figure 16.3.

Lesson 16

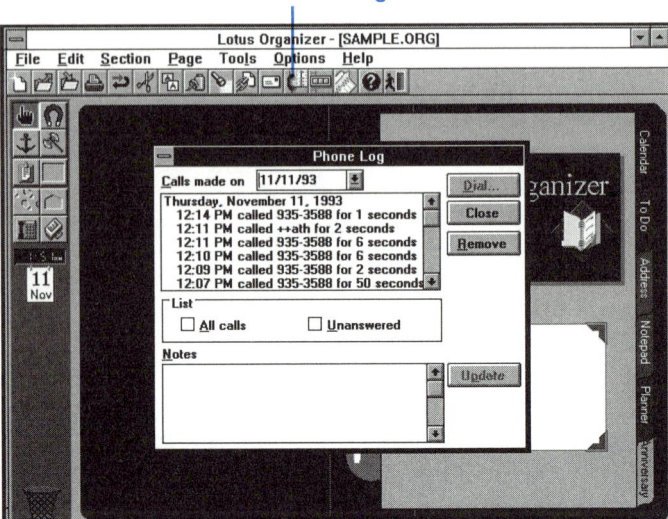

Figure 16.3 The Phone Log dialog box.

3. If you want to tell the Phone Log dialog box to display calls made on another date, click on the down-arrow button next to the **C**alls made on text box to display a Calendar. Click on any other date to see the contents of that day's phone log.

4. If the list of calls is too long to be visible, use the vertical scroll bar to review more calls.

5. Click on the All calls check box to see every call made on the selected date.

6. Click on the Unanswered check box to see a list of calls that went unanswered on the selected day. The logged reason for the unanswered call will appear next to the phone call listed.

Logging and Tracking Phone Calls

7. If you kept notes of any of your logged phoned calls, they'll appear in the **Notes** dialog box when you highlight that phone call on the list. Figure 16.4 shows you an example of notes taken during a phone conversation.

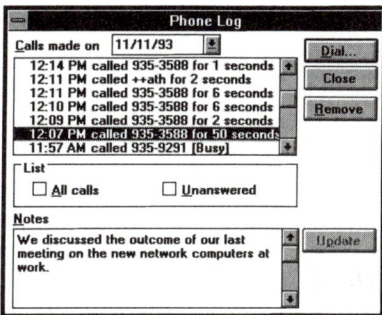

Figure 16.4 Notes taken during a logged phone call.

8. Click on the **Remove** button to delete a call from your Phone Log.

If you changed any text taken during a phone conversation, you should click on the **Update** button to save your changes. Click on the **Dial** button to dial a selected phone number. Click on the **Close** button to close the Phone Log dialog box.

> **Your Call** Double-click on any call listed to dial that number.

In this lesson, you learned how to dial, log, and track phone numbers. In the next lesson, you'll learn how to work with Organizer's Anniversary section.

Lesson 17

Working with Anniversaries

In this lesson, you'll learn about Organizer's Anniversary section. You'll learn how to fill Organizer's Anniversary section with information about personal and business anniversaries.

What Is an Anniversary?

Everyone—and I mean *everyone*—forgets an anniversary now and then. (Let's hope that the one you forget belongs to someone else.) With Lotus Organizer, you don't have to blow off those important dates any more. You can keep a special diary of Anniversaries. In fact, any event that recurs annually (birthdays, trade shows, office parties, and so on) can be tracked with Organizer's Anniversary section.

The handiest thing about the Anniversary section is the fact that you can review anniversaries on a monthly basis—you don't have to check the Anniversary section every day. The ability to see all anniversaries for an entire month at-a-glance is the biggest, single benefit to using the Anniversary section versus the Calendar section. The Anniversary section is made up of a dozen lists. (Each of the lists represents a different month.) The entries you make in the Anniversary section show up in your Calendar section along with your appointments.

Working with Anniversaries   87

Adding an Anniversary

Here's how to add an anniversary to your Anniversary section:

1. Open your Organizer file.

2. Click on the Anniversary section tab. Figure 17.1 shows you the sample Anniversary section found in SAMPLE.ORG.

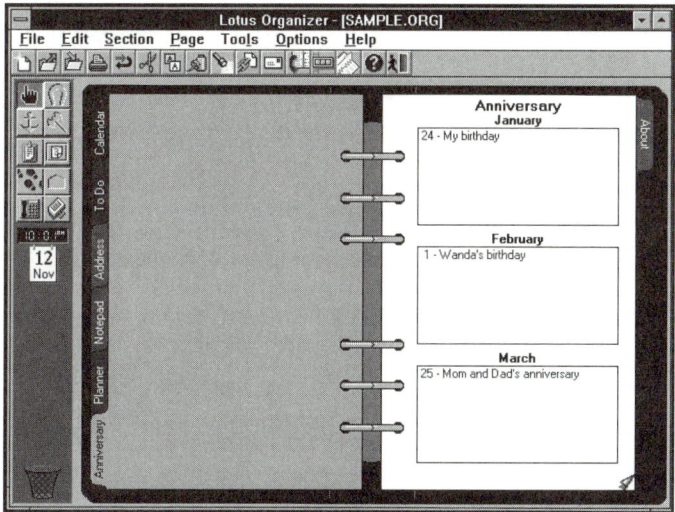

Figure 17.1   The Anniversary section.

3. Use the Page Up and Page Down keys to flip through the pages until you can see the month you want.

   > **Shortcut**   You can also click on the lower-outside edge of each page of your Anniversary section to turn its pages.

4. Click on an empty space in the month when the Anniversary occurs. The Anniversary dialog box will open, shown in Figure 17.2.

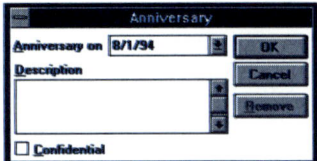

Figure 17.2   The Anniversary dialog box.

5. Select a date in the **A**nniversary on text box. You can type a date into the text box, or you can click on the down-arrow button to choose a date from the calendar display. Change months in the calendar display by clicking on either black arrow. Select a day of the month by clicking on that day's number.

6. In the **D**escription text box, type the text that will serve as a description for this anniversary. Your description text can contain up to 256 characters.

7. Click on the OK button to commit your Anniversary text to Organizer's Anniversary section.

> **Nice Try!**   Don't expect to be able to make a list in the **D**escription text box. You can use the Ctrl+Enter keys to begin a new line in the **D**escription text box, but it will be displayed as a single, long sentence when it's shown in the Anniversary section.

Changing an Anniversary

There will always be times when you find an Anniversary entry is inaccurate for one reason or another. Sometimes, we type badly; sometimes we misspell the names of people mentioned in our Anniversary Descriptions. Whatever the cause, corrections can often be in order.

Working with Anniversaries

You can change the text in the Description of any Anniversary. You can also change the date of any Anniversary. Here's how:

1. Open the Anniversary section.

2. Use the Page Up and Page Down keys to flip through the pages until you can see the month that holds the Anniversary you want to change.

> **Or . . .** You can also click on the lower-outside edge of each page of your Anniversary section to turn its pages, or select **P**rior Page or **N**ext Page from the **P**age menu.

3. Click on the anniversary that you want to change. The Anniversary dialog box will open.

4. If you want to change the date, click on the down-arrow button next to the **A**nniversary on text box, and choose a new date. If you want to change the Description text, click inside the **D**escription text box and change your text.

5. Click on the OK button when you're through.

Your Anniversary section will now display your changes. If you've changed the date, you may have to flip through the pages to the new month in order to see the anniversary.

Deleting an Anniversary

Sometimes, people leave your life for one reason or another. Things constantly change. On occasion, you might have to delete anniversaries. Here's how to delete an anniversary:

1. Open the Anniversary section.

2. Navigate to the anniversary you want to delete.

3. Drag-and-drop the defunct anniversary onto the Trash icon.

The pointer changes to indicate that you are using drag-and-drop while you drag an anniversary to the Trash.

Trash Day   You can't undo the deletion of an anniversary that's been dragged into the Trash!

In this lesson, you learned how to work with your Anniversary section. In the next lesson, you'll learn how to print information found in your Organizer file.

Lesson 18

Printing

In this lesson, you'll learn about printing the information in your Organizer file.

Printing Sections of the Organizer

Organizer lets you print the contents of your different sections, which means you can have actual hard copy pages to be inserted into your day planner or generate mailing labels. The process of printing from all of Organizer's sections is fairly universal. You can use the same dialog box to print all of the sections.

> **I Know That!** Of course, you need to make sure that you've installed a printer driver that matches the printer connected to your computer. See your documentation for more details.

To print a section, follow these instructions:

1. Open the Organizer file you want to use.

2. Select Print from the File menu, or click on the Print icon in the Toolbox. The Print dialog box will open, as shown in Figure 18.1.

Lesson 18

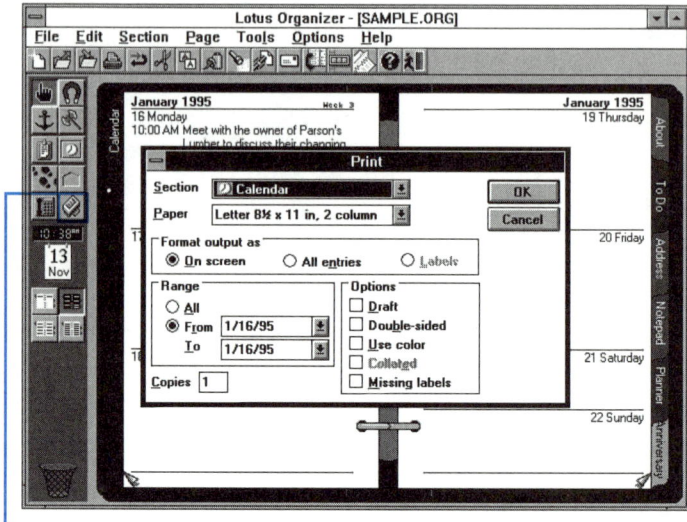

Print icon

Figure 18.1 The Print dialog box.

3. In the Section drop-down list box, choose the section you want to print.

4. In the Paper drop-down list box, select the paper size you will be using.

5. In the Copies text box, type in the number of copies you want.

6. Select OK. The specified section will print.

As shown in Figure 18.1, there are several other options in the Print dialog box. For example, you can print certain pages of a section, you can print labels, or you can print double-sided pages. If you want to take advantage of some of these options, follow these instructions:

1. Click on the section tab for the section you want to print from.

2. Navigate to the page you want to print.

Printing   93

3. Select Print from the File menu, or click on the Print icon in the Toolbox.

4. To print a certain portion of a section:

- Under Format output as, make sure On screen is selected.
- Under Range, make sure the From and To dates are correct.

5. To change print options:

- Select the Draft check box if you don't want the printout to be letter quality.
- Select Double-sided if you want the printout to use both sides of the page.
- Choose Use color if you have a color printer and you want a color printout.
- Select Collated if you are printing more than one copy and you want the copies collated.
- Choose Missing labels if you've already used some of the labels from the sheet of labels you're printing on.

Something's Missing If your printouts aren't showing enough information, you might need to change the view of the section before you print. Click on one of the view buttons below the Toolbox to change views.

Be Specific! If you want to print a specific address, appointment, or Notepad page, you can just drag-and-drop it onto the Print icon in the Toolbox.

Lesson 18

Printing Labels

Organizer comes equipped to print standard label formats to suit the most readily available label stock. However, you can only print labels from the Notepad and Address sections. That's because label printing really doesn't make sense when you're working with a chart in the Planner section, for example.

> **Don't Settle for Less** You can customize any label's layout, if you want. Check out Lesson 19 for more on creating customized label layouts.

Here's how you print labels:

1. Open an Organizer file.

2. If you're using a special printer to print the labels, choose Printer Setup from the File menu, and select the correct printer.

3. Select Print from the File menu, or click on the Print icon in the Toolbox. The Print dialog box will open.

4. Select the section from which you want to print labels. If you're just going through a dry run at this point, try selecting the Address section.

5. Next, select the label format you want to use. Pay particular attention to the dimensions of the label you select. Click on the down-arrow button next to the Paper text box to review, and select one of the available label formats.

6. Click on the Labels option button under Format output as.

7. Click on the All option button to print every address in your section, or if you want to limit printing to a

range of names, click on the From option button. Type in the first name to go on the labels in the From text box, and type in the last name to be printed in the To text box. Be sure to overwrite the ">" symbol in the text boxes.

8. Enter the number of copies you want to print in the Copies text box.

9. Select from the list of printing options under Options.

10. Click on the OK button to begin printing labels.

In this lesson, you learned how to print. In the next lesson, you'll learn how to customize Organizer.

Lesson 19

Customizing Page Layout

In this lesson, you'll learn how to customize Organizer's pages. You'll learn how to select a font and prepare a label's layout to suit your own needs.

Choosing a Page Layout

When you are ready to print information, you will want to make sure that the paper you're printing on is the type and size for your needs. You might want to print your addresses onto small Rolodex cards. You may also want to print the same addresses on the larger Rolodex cards for someone who uses them in that size and format. All you have to do is change the page layout before you print.

You can change the page layout for any Organizer information you want to print. Organizer comes equipped with several common page layout forms intended for use with paper products that are available at your local office supply store.

Here's how you change the page layout:

1. Open an Organizer file.

2. Select Page Setup from the File menu. The Paper Layouts dialog box will open, like the one shown in Figure 19.1.

Customizing Page Layout

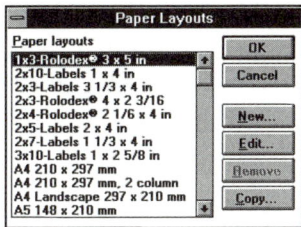

Figure 19.1 The Paper Layouts dialog box.

3. Click on one of the paper layouts offered in the **P**aper layouts list box. Use the vertical scroll bar to review the entire list, if you want.

4. Click on the OK button once you've made your choice.

Organizer remembers the most recently selected paper layout, so until you change it again, you'll be printing on the paper layout you chose last.

> **It Gets Easier!** You can also change to another *stock* paper layout in the **P**aper Layouts dialog box.

Changing the Page Setup

You have the option to change all of Organizer's paper layouts. You can choose from one of the default layouts, or you can opt to customize a label's layout for your own purposes.

Here's how you change the setup of a page:

1. Select Page Setup from the File menu. The Paper Layouts dialog box will open.

Lesson 19

Shortcut! Double-click on one of the existing paper layouts offered in the **P**aper layouts list box to change your layout if you don't want to create a new layout from a copy of an existing one.

2. Single-click on one of the existing layouts displayed in the **P**aper layouts list box. Use the vertical scroll bar to review the entire list if you don't see the one you want.

3. Click on the Copy button to create a copy of the selected page layout. The Page Setup dialog box will open. The dialog box for the 1x3-Rolodex 3 x 5 in. is shown in Figure 19.2.

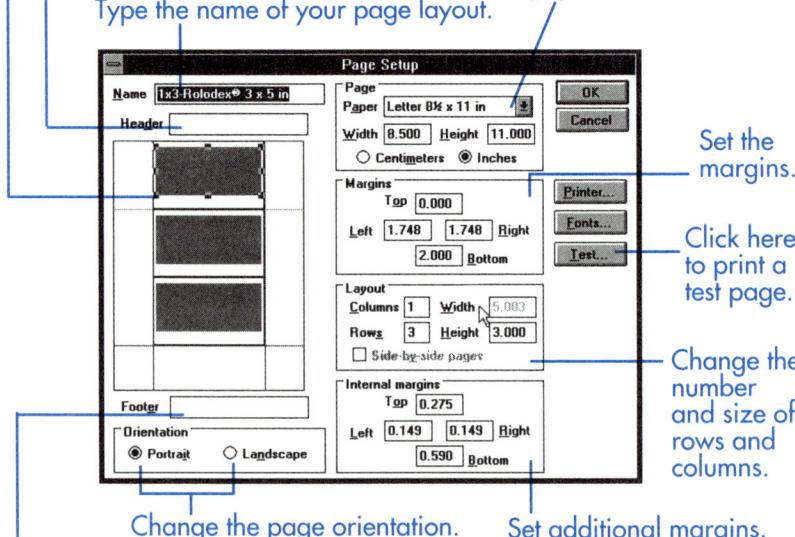

Figure 19.2 The Page Setup dialog box.

Customizing Page Layout   99

Note that you can't change some of the information in a page layout that's provided with Organizer by default.

4. Choose the options you want from the dialog box.

For a list of the Header and Footer commands used to print, see your documentation.

5. Click on the OK button to save your new page layout and add it to the list of other page layouts displayed in the **P**aper layouts text box.

If you scroll through the list of page layouts displayed in the Paper Layouts dialog box, you'll see that paper layouts you create are added to the list of layouts. Figure 19.3 shows you a new page layout added to the list.

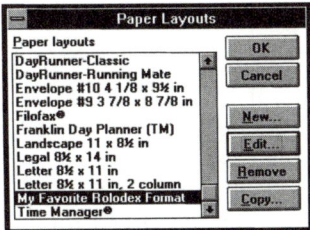

Figure 19.3   ***My Favorite Rolodex Format*** is added to the list.

Selecting a Font

Sometimes it's just a personal preference. Other times, it's a requirement of your department or business system. For whatever reason, you'll probably find yourself changing the fonts used for the printing of Organizer information. You can use any font you've installed on your computer.

Lesson 19

Here's how you select a font:

1. Select Page Setup from the File menu. The Paper Layouts dialog box will open.

2. When the Paper Layouts dialog box opens, click on the layout you want, and then click on the Edit button.

3. In the Page Setup dialog box, click on the Fonts button to open the Font Mapping dialog box shown in Figure 19.4.

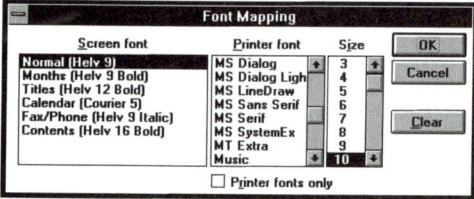

Figure 19.4 The Font Mapping dialog box.

4. If you want information printed using the fonts as displayed by each section (shown in parentheses next to each item on the list), click on the Printer fonts only check box.

5. If you want to assign another font, select one from the **P**rinter font list box, and then select any available size from those displayed in the S**i**ze list box.

> **Make It Easier** As always, you can use the Tab key to toggle between the list boxes and buttons in this dialog box. Toggling with the Tab key is a great way to find an elusive highlight.

6. Close all the open dialog boxes.

The Way It Was You can always click on the Clear button to restore the original default font selections.

In this lesson, you learned how to customize the page layout of labels. In the next lesson, you'll learn how to customize Organizer even further by changing the color of Organizer's binder, creating or changing passwords, and more.

Lesson

Using a Password

In this lesson, you'll learn how to set and change a password.

Establishing a Password

Organizer helps you keep unauthorized people from viewing and changing your Organizer files. This level of security is maintained by the use of password protection. There are three levels of password protection that you can use after you establish your own personal password.

Follow these guidelines when selecting a password:

- A *private* password allows anyone who knows it to add, edit, and delete any information, including data marked confidential.

- A *public* password provides add, edit, and delete rights to the user. A public password will not allow the user to see confidential information. A public password does allow a user to make his or her own added information confidential.

- A *read only* password allows the user to see only nonconfidential information. The user cannot add, edit, or delete the information he/she sees.

Here's how you establish a password:

1. Open an Organizer file.

2. Select Passwords from the File menu. The Passwords dialog box will open, as shown in Figure 20.1.

Using a Password

Figure 20.1 The Passwords dialog box.

3. Type your password into the **Pri**vate text box. Notice that asterisks are substituted for the characters you type to prevent clandestine on-lookers from learning your password.

> **Be Careful!** Organizer's passwords are case sensitive. If you establish a password with any uppercase letters, you'll have to uppercase those same letters every time you use your password.

4. If you want others to use a password different from your own, place the insertion point in the P**u**blic text box, and type the password that you want others to use. Do the same with the **R**ead only text box.

5. Click on the OK button, and retype the same information into the Retype the passwords dialog box.

6. Click on the OK button to close the dialog box.

You now have password protection for information maintained in any of your Organizer's sections.

Changing a Password

There will be times when you need to change a password. If an unauthorized person should find out one of your three passwords, you can change any of the current passwords to re-establish security.

Lesson 20

Here's how you change a password:

1. Select Passwords from the File menu. The Passwords dialog box will open.

Say the Secret Password If you want to change a password, you have to *retype* all three of them, but you don't have to *change* all three.

2. If you want to change the private password, type over the asterisks in the Private text box.

3. If necessary, retype the passwords in the other two text boxes.

4. Click on the OK button, and retype the same information into the Retype the passwords dialog box.

5. Click on the OK button to close the dialog box.

Unless you made a mistake, your information should now be protected with your new password(s). The next time someone tries to open your Organizer file, he or she will be presented with the dialog box shown in Figure 20.2.

Figure 20.2 Organizer asks the user for the password before it opens the file.

If an unauthorized person tries to gain entry to your password-protected Organizer file, he or she will see the dialog box shown in Figure 20.3.

Using a Password

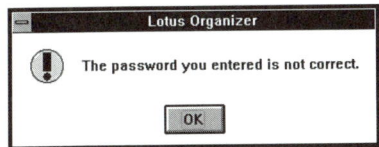

Figure 20.3 How embarrassing!

In this lesson, you learned how to set and change a password. In the next lesson, you'll learn how to customize Organizer.

Lesson 21

Customizing Organizer

In this lesson, you'll learn about customizing Organizer's screen. You'll also learn how to change display colors and customize other display preferences.

Putting Your Name on Your Organizer

You should take a moment to personalize your Organizer. Since Organizer uses the metaphor of the traditional daily planner, your name should go on the front cover for all to see. You have seven lines of text space to work with.

Here's how to put your name on your Organizer:

1. Open the Organizer file so the front page of the binder is showing.

2. Place the insertion point in the name tag area.

3. Type the name you want to appear on the front of the binder. You can use arrow keys, the space bar, and the Delete key to navigate around the name tag while you're personalizing.

4. When finished, select Save from the File menu.

Changing the Color of the Binder

If you're one of those people who just has to see software display their favorite colors, you're in luck. You can change the color of the binder to suit your personal preference.

Customizing Organizer

This is how you change the color of Organizer's binder:

1. Choose Display from the Options menu. The Display dialog box will open, like the one shown in Figure 21.1.

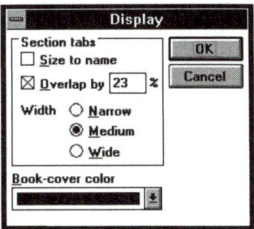

Figure 21.1 The Display dialog box.

2. Click on the down-arrow button next to the **Book-cover color** list box to see a list of the available colors for your binder. You can use the vertical scroll bar to see all of the colors.

3. Click on the color you want.

4. Click on the OK button to close the Display dialog box.

Your binder should now be the color you chose. The same color will be displayed when you open the Organizer file again.

Setting Display Preferences

You have the option to enable or disable the display of the date and time below the Toolbox. Also, certain file saving features can be enabled or disabled. In addition, you can choose to use Organizer in monochrome view if you have a *paper white monitor*. You can even disable or enable the animated page-turning that you see when you flip through the pages of one of Organizer's sections.

Lesson 21

Paper White Monitor A monitor that displays shades of gray instead of colors.

Here's how you customize Organizer's preferences:

1. Select Preferences from the Options menu. The Preferences dialog box shown in Figure 21.2 will open.

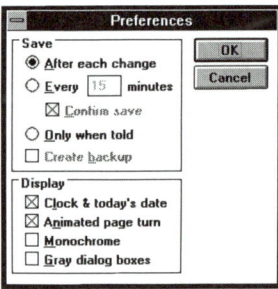

Figure 21.2 The Preferences dialog box.

2. Enable or disable these options in the Save group box:

- Click on the After each change option button to cause Organizer to automatically save any changes you make. Or click on the Every *xx* minutes option box, and enter a length of time to wait between saves.

- You can make Organizer ask you if it's okay to save before it does so. Click on the Confirm save check box to make Organizer ask you.

- Click on the Only when told option button to disable automatic file saving features. When this option is disabled, you can save your changes by selecting Save from the File menu.

Customizing Organizer 109

- Click on the Create backup check box to force Organizer to create a backup file with the file name extension of .BAK every time a file is saved.

3. These next options appear in the Display group box:

- Click on the Clock & today's date check box if you want to see the date and time displayed below the Toolbox on Organizer's screen.

- Click on the Animated page turn check box if you want to see Organizer's page-flipping action.

- Click on the Monochrome check box if you want to see Organizer change its shades of color to work more effectively with a monochrome monitor. If you have a color VGA monitor, you won't see any change when you select this option.

- Click on the Gray dialog boxes check box if you want to see gray 3-D dialog boxes instead of the traditional 2-D black-on-white ones. (Figure 21.3 shows you an example of what dialog boxes will look like when this check box is enabled.) This option is not available if you selected the Monochrome check box.

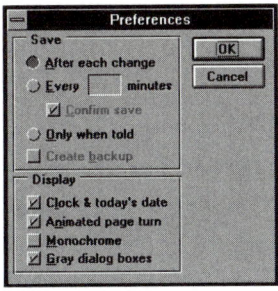

Figure 21.3 An example gray dialog box.

Lesson 21

In this lesson, you learned how to customize Organizer's screen and file saving features to suit your own needs. In the next lesson, you'll learn how to use a modem to Autodial phone numbers.

Lesson 22

Using the Autodialer

In this lesson, you'll learn how to use Organizer's Autodialer in conjunction with the Address section.

What Is the Autodialer?

Organizer's Autodialer is a special utility that helps you maintain a phone log and lets you dial any phone numbers in your address book as well as any number in your phone log. You can also fine-tune Organizer's Autodialer to suit your own needs. You can dial phone numbers that are internal to your own telephone system, such as your colleagues' extension numbers. You can use special internal phone system codes to gain outside line or outbound watts line access.

Making a Phone Call

You can use Organizer's Autodialer to do just about anything related to your phone calls—everything except talk on the phone for you! You will probably find that you'll soon be spoiled by the Autodialer's ease-of-use.

Here's how you make a phone call with Autodialer:

1. Open an Organizer file.

2. Select Phone Call from the Tools menu, or click on the Phone icon in the Toolbox. The Dial dialog box, shown in Figure 22.1, will open.

Lesson 22

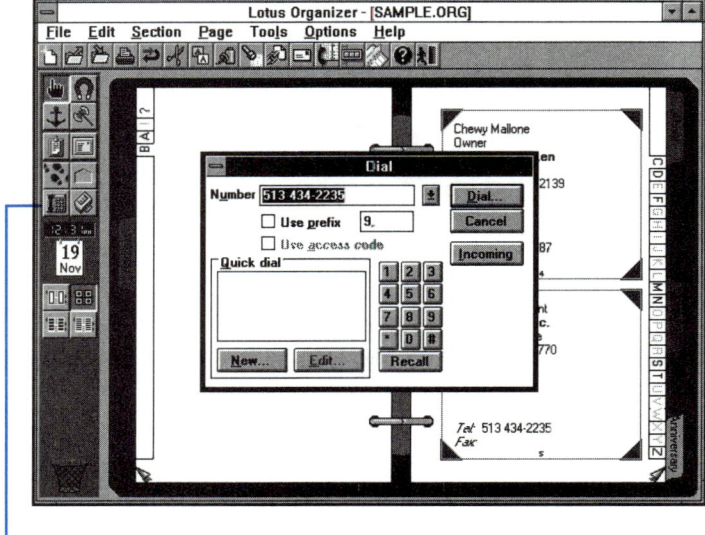
Phone icon

Figure 22.1 The Dial dialog box.

Speed Dialing If you want to dial a phone number located in your Address section, go to that address in the Address section, and then drag-and-drop the address onto the Phone icon in the Toolbox.

3. Enter a phone number into the **N**umber text box. (If you dragged an address onto the Phone icon, you'll see a phone number already placed in the Number text box.)

4. Click on the Use prefix check box if you want Autodialer to dial the number in the text box before the phone number. Use any long distance or outside-line access code here.

Using the Autodialer

Take a Break Place a comma after each code to cause Autodialer to pause after each code used. Pausing between codes helps the phone system to keep up with Autodialer.

5. If you've enabled the use of a default access code, you can click on the Use access code check box to cause Autodialer to use it.

6. If you have dialed numbers in the past, they'll be displayed in the **Q**uick dial list box. Double-click on one to place the phone number in the **Nu**mber text box.

7. Click on the Dial button to place your call.

When you click on the Dial button, you'll see the Dial dialog box open. If you want to log the results of the call, click on one of the buttons displayed, and then leave yourself a note to be kept in your phone log.

Reviewing the Phone Log

You can review the information stored in your phone log in case you want to use a phone number again. The Phone Log allows you to review any calls made on a certain date. Remember, you have to commit the results of your calls to the Phone Log in order to review them later. (For more information on logging phone calls, turn back to Lesson 16.)

Here's how you review your Phone Log:

1. Select Phone Log from the Tools menu. The Phone Log dialog box will open, shown in Figure 22.2. Note that the Phone Log shows your calls for today's date only (if you've logged any).

Lesson 22

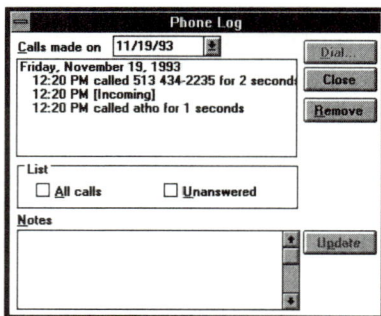

Figure 22.2 The Phone Log dialog box.

2. If you want to select another date for review, click on the down-arrow button next to the Calls made on text box.

3. A vertical scroll bar will appear if your Phone Log contains too many logged entries to fit in the list box. Use the vertical scroll bar to see all of your calls in the Phone Log for the date selected.

4. If you want to review logged Notes for a call, click on that call to see notes displayed in the Notes text box. Once you click on a listed call, you can then click on the Dial button to initiate another call.

5. Click on the All calls check box if you want to see all calls for all dates.

6. Click on the Unanswered check box if you just want to see calls that were logged as unanswered.

7. Click on the Close button to end your review of your Phone Log.

You can remove an entry from your Phone Log if you click on the unwanted entry and then click on the Remove button.

Using the Autodialer

Setting Autodialer Preferences

You can preset Autodialer preferences at any time. Autodialer preferences are optional. You don't have to fuss with them to use Autodialer, but you may find that you can save time and energy by changing these options to suit your individual needs.

1. Select Autodialer from the Options menu. The Autodialer Options dialog box will open, as shown in Figure 22.3.

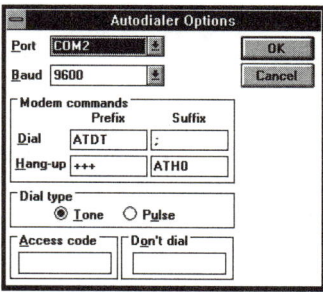

Figure 22.3 The Autodialer Options dialog box.

2. Your modem is configured to work with a particular *port* on your computer. You should make sure that the port displayed matches the port that's used by your modem.

> **Port** One of the four available serial communications channels provided on many computers. Your own computer may be configured with less than four.

3. Select a *Baud rate* that matches the maximum achievable with your modem. (Select the highest Baud setting if you're not sure which one is right for you.)

Baud Rate The working rate of speed that can be accomplished by a modem.

4. You should be using a Hayes-compatible modem with Organizer's Autodialer. The setting displayed in the Modem commands group box reflects the use of a Hayes-compatible modem. You can change some of the commands used to manage your modem.

Modem Mania If your modem is Autodialing properly, don't change any of these settings! If your modem is not dialing when it should, refer to your modem's manual to make sure that the four text boxes in the Modem commands group box contain commands that match the proper ones to use with your particular modem.

5. Click on either the Tone or Pulse option buttons to reflect the type of telephone system you have.

6. If you always have to use an access code to dial your phone, enter it into the Access code text box so you don't have to manually type it in every time you dial.

7. Type your own area code into the Don't dial text box if you have phone numbers in your Address section that include your own area code. (Some regional telephone systems don't allow the use of your own area code in a dialing sequence.)

8. Click on the OK button to close the Autodialer Options dialog box.

In this lesson, you learned how to work with Organizer's Autodialer and the Phone Log. In the next lesson, you'll learn how to link Organizer information to files originated by other applications.

Lesson 23

Using Links to Cross Reference Information

In this lesson, you'll learn how to keep information automatically updated (linked) between sections of your Organizer files and with the files of other applications.

What Are Links?

Links are connections between Organizer sections. Organizer allows you to cross-reference (link) information maintained by some sections of Organizer. You can use these links to quickly jump to a certain Notepad page or a specific entry in your Address book. Links are a neat way to see related information in other Organizer sections or another application's files. You can set up a whole network of linked information.

Linking information is a great way to network diverse information, for example, a group of individuals working on the same project. If you are a member of a group, such as a council, board, or committee, you can establish a link to every other member of your group so you can jump between their entries in the Address book without having to remember their names. Linking these people would make the task of contacting each of them a simple one.

Setting Up Links

You have to set up a link before you can use it to jump quickly to another Organizer section's information or another application's file.

Link It You can link information between any of Organizer's sections except Planner and Anniversary.

Here's how you set up a link:

1. Open an Organizer file.

2. Open the Organizer section that holds the information that's to be linked to information elsewhere. You must be looking at your information in order to set up a Link.

3. Click on the Link button in the Toolbox. It looks like a ship's anchor. When you click on the Link button, an anchor icon will appear next to your mouse pointer.

4. Click on the information you want to link. Figure 23.1 shows you an example of information selected for linking. Note that a chain is now added to the anchor.

5. Navigate to the information that will comprise the other end of the link. In Figure 23.2, I've selected the address of a computer consultant in the Address section.

6. Click on the information to be linked. A link of chain will be displayed near the linked information to signify that a link has been established, as shown in Figure 23.3.

Using Links to Cross Reference Information   119

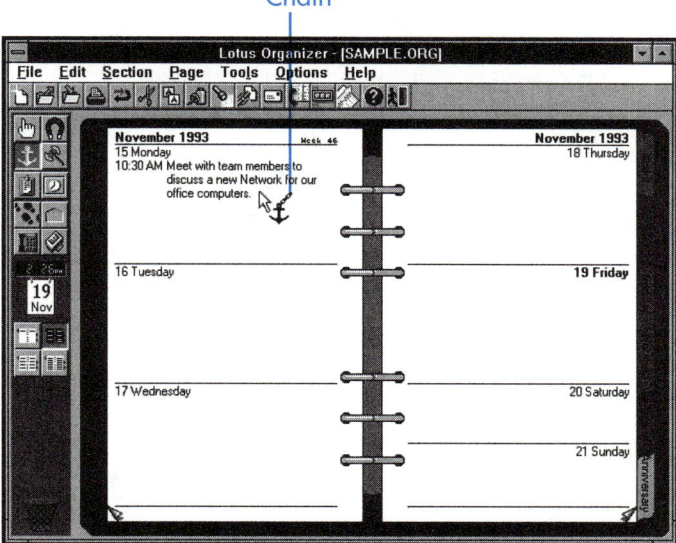

Figure 23.1 The chain signifies the first part of the Link.

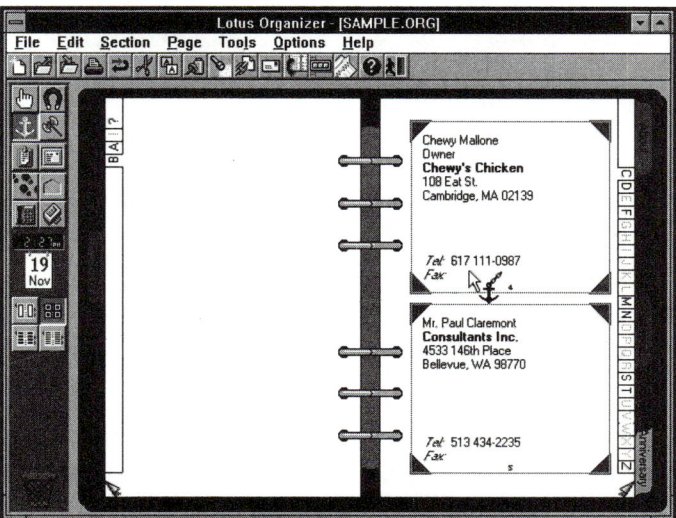

Figure 23.2 The information that is the other end of the Link.

Lesson 23

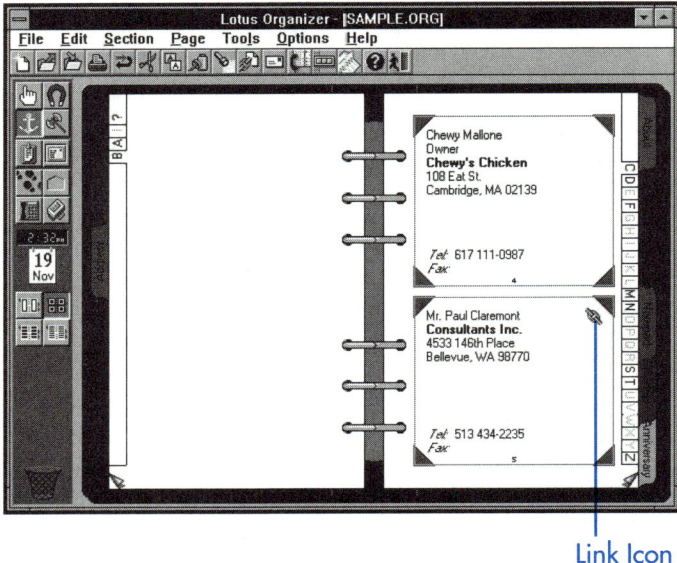

Link Icon

Figure 23.3 The Link icon.

7. Click on the Pointer tool in the Toolbox to complete the link and return the pointer to its normal state. Your link is now established.

To see your newly linked information, point to the Link icon and hold down the left mouse button. To jump to the other end of your Link, move the pointer over the Link information, and release the left mouse button.

Using Multiple Links

You can link more than two pieces of information. You can link several bits of detail to a single one, or you can link one piece of information to several single entries. The number of links that can be created is entirely up to you. In this set of steps, you'll link another entry to a link already established.

Here's how you set up and use multiple links:

Using Links to Cross Reference Information

1. Open the Organizer section holding the information that's already been linked. Just as in establishing a single link, you must be looking at information in order to set up multiple links.

2. Navigate to a piece of information that's already been linked.

3. Click on the Link button in Organizer's Toolbox. An anchor icon will appear next to your mouse pointer.

4. Hold down the Ctrl key while you click on the information already linked. Linked information displays a link of chain nearby.

5. Navigate to and click on the information that will comprise the other end of this new multiple link. A link of chain will be displayed near the newly linked information to signify that a link has been established.

6. Click on the Pointer tool in the Toolbox to complete the link.

To see your multiple, newly linked information, point to the Link icon that appears on any of the three linked pieces of information and hold down the left mouse button. You'll see one link beside an arrow icon. Move the pointer onto that arrow icon to open the Link menu. The Link menu is made up of the multiple links you create. When you add new links they are added to the Link menu as menu items.

To jump to the other end of any multiple link, move the pointer over the Link menu item that represents the information you want to see, and then release the left mouse button.

Lesson 23

Using Information from Other Applications

You can link information in one of your sections with other applications' files. You could, for example, open a spreadsheet file that relates to a meeting described in an appointment.

Here's how you establish a link to another application's file:

1. Open the Organizer section holding the information you want to link. You must be looking at information in order to link it.

2. Click on the Link button in Organizer's Toolbox. An anchor icon will appear next to your mouse pointer.

3. Click on the information you want to link. A chain will be added to the anchor that appears next to the mouse pointer.

4. Select Reference from the File menu. The Reference dialog box will open, like the one shown in Figure 23.4.

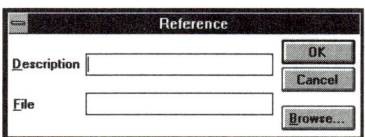

Figure 23.4 The Reference dialog box.

5. In the **D**escription text box, type the name you want to use as a label for this link.

6. If you know the name of the file that contains the information that will comprise the other end of

Using Links to Cross Reference Information 123

your link, type it into the **File** text box. If you don't know the exact path and file name, click on the **Browse** button to search for it.

7. Click on the **OK** button to close the reference dialog box.

8. Click on the **Pointer** icon in the Toolbox to complete the linking process.

Your link has now been established. A Link icon will appear near the Organizer information that you linked. To see your new external link as it's listed on the Link menu, point to the Link icon, and hold down the left mouse button. Figure 23.5 shows you a single external link listed on the Link menu.

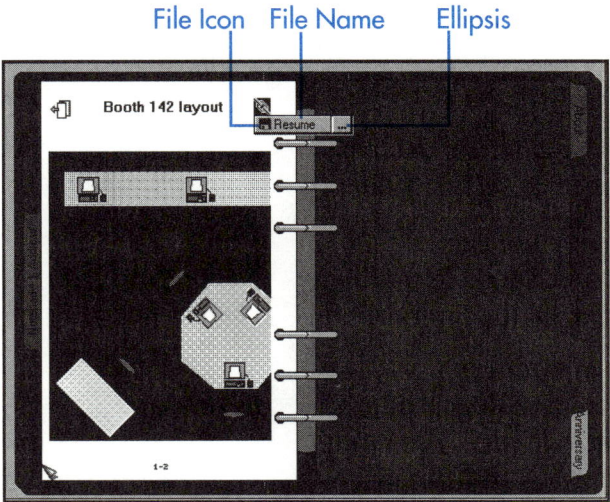

Figure 23.5 A single external link on the Link menu.

Linked application files are represented on the Link menu by a small diskette icon and the name of the file. The Link menu will appear when you click and hold the mouse button while pointing to this new link icon.

Lesson 23

To see what you typed into the Reference dialog box, move the pointer over the ellipsis (...) at the end of the Link menu item, and release the mouse button.

To jump to the other end of your Link, move the pointer over the Link information, and release the left mouse button.

In this lesson, you learned how to link information between Organizer's sections and how to link Organizer with information created by external applications. In the next lesson, you'll learn how to save damaged files and how to save disk space.

Lesson 24

Using Organizer Utilities

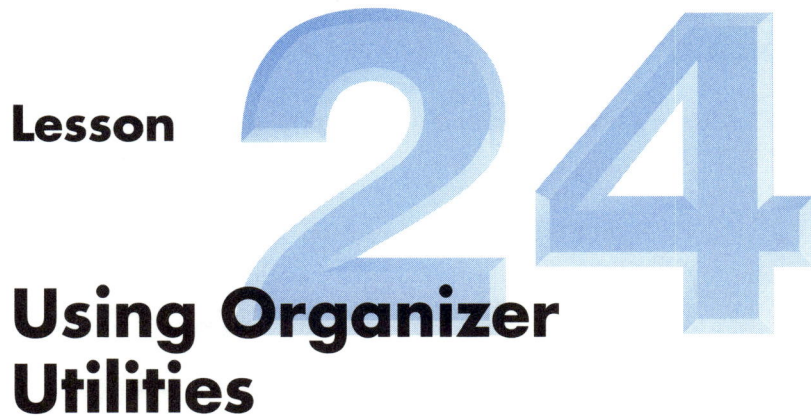

In this lesson, you'll learn how to save files that have been damaged and how to compact Organizer files to save disk space.

What Are the Organizer Utilities?

The Organizer Utilities are designed to recover a file damaged by misuse or mistake. If Organizer won't open an Organizer file for you, the chances are that it's damaged and in need of repair. You can also use the Utilities to compact any Organizer file. This lesson will show you how to run the Organizer Utilities and use them to compact or recover files.

Saving a Damaged File

Organizer will tell you when you have an Organizer file that's in need of repair. Organizer will tell you about your problem when you try to open the damaged file. You'll see a dialog box like the one shown in Figure 24.1.

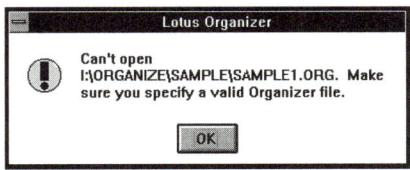

Figure 24.1 News of a damaged Organizer file.

Lesson 24

Here's how you repair a damaged Organizer file:

1. Start Organizer.

2. Click on the Control-menu box. The Control menu will open.

3. Select Run. The Run Program dialog box will open.

4. Double-click on the Organizer Utilities option button. The Lotus Organizer Utilities dialog box will open.

5. Click on the Open button to open the Open File dialog box.

6. Navigate to the Organizer file of interest, and double-click on it to close the Open File dialog box.

The Organizer Utilities will now check the selected Organizer file for errors. If the Organizer Utilities finds that the file is damaged, you'll be shown a dialog box like the one in Figure 24.2.

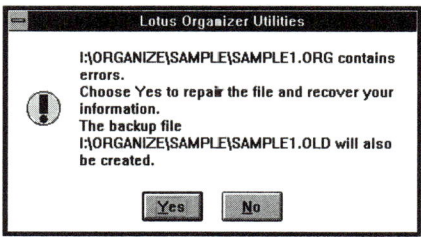

Figure 24.2 You're prompted to begin the repair process.

Click on the Yes button to begin the repair of the file. If the selected Organizer file is not corrupted, you'll see the Status dialog box. It advises you of the progress made in repairing your Organizer file.

Using Organizer Utilities 127

Shrink It! Always compact a file when prompted to do so by the Organizer Utilities. The compacting process not only saves space, but it also reorganizes the file, resulting in optimum safety for your Organizer information.

If the Organizer Utilities finds information in the damaged Organizer file that doesn't seem to fit anywhere within the file, it will suggest exporting the information so you can review it later and re-enter it if needed. Let the Organizer Utilities export the *unreferenced records* by clicking on the Yes button.

Sorry! If the file can't be saved, you'll see a dialog box that tells you so. There's nothing you can do.

When information is exported during the repair process, a file is created with a file name that reflects the Organizer section it came from, with a file name extension of CSV (such as :ADDRESS.CSV). You can review the contents of this CSV file with any file viewer utility, or even Windows' Notepad. You can now import that CSV file back into your Organizer. See Lesson 15 for more about importing records into an Organizer section.

Compacting a File

If you chose to compact a file during the process of saving a damaged file, the Organizer Utilities will tell you how many bytes were saved by compacting the file. Figure 24.3 shows you an example of the potential disk space savings for a sample Organizer file. Your savings will vary with the size of your Organizer file. When you're done marveling at the space saved, click on the OK button to close this dialog box.

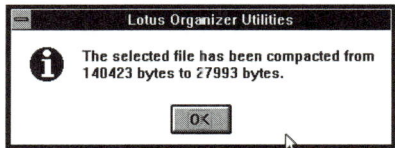

Figure 24.3 The space that can be saved by compacting!

The Lotus Organizer Utilities dialog box will display a list of the information in your Organizer file. Click on any item in the Section list box to review details relating to the selection. The details will be displayed in the Information list box. Click on the Save button to save your work, and then click on the Exit button to close the Organizer Utilities.

In this lesson, you learned all about using the Organizer Utilities to free up disk space and save damaged Organizer files. Please refer to the following appendix if you need a refresher course in Windows.

Appendix A

Windows Basics

Tell Me About Windows

Microsoft Windows is a graphical interface program that makes your computer easier to use by enabling you to select menu items and pictures rather than type commands. Before you can take advantage of it, however, you must learn some Windows basics.

Starting Microsoft Windows

To start Windows, do the following:

1. At the DOS prompt, type **win**.

2. Press Enter.

The Windows title screen appears for a few moments, and then you see a screen like the one in Figure A.1.

> **What If It Didn't Work?** You may have to change to the windows directory before starting Windows; to do so, type **CD \WINDOWS** and press Enter.

Appendix A

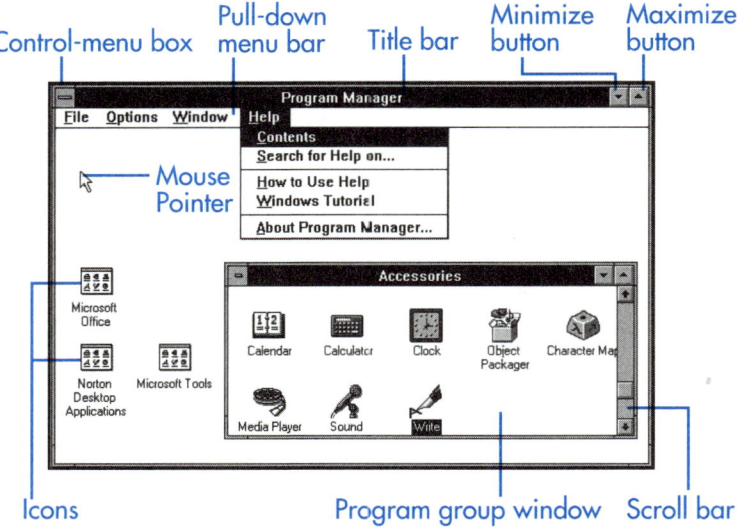

Figure A.1 The Windows Program Manager.

Parts of a Windows Screen

As shown in Figure A.1, the Windows screen contains several unique elements that you won't see in DOS. Here's a brief summary:

- *Title bar*   Shows the name of the window or program.

- *Program group windows*   Contain program icons which allow you to run programs.

- *Icons*   Graphic representations of programs. To run a program, you select its icon.

- *Minimize and Maximize buttons*   Alter a window's size. The Minimize button shrinks the window to the size of an icon. The Maximize button expands the window to fill the screen. When maximized, a window contains a double-arrow *Restore* button, which returns the window to its original size.

Windows Basics 131

- *Control-menu box* When selected, pulls down a menu that offers size and location controls for the window.

- *Pull-down menu bar* Contains a list of the pull-down menus available in the program.

- *Mouse Pointer* If you are using a mouse, the mouse pointer (usually an arrow) appears on-screen. It can be controlled by moving the mouse (discussed later in this appendix).

- *Scroll bars* If a window contains more information than can be displayed in the window, a scroll bar appears. *Scroll arrows* on each end of the scroll bar allow you to scroll slowly. The *scroll box* allows you to scroll more quickly.

Using a Mouse

To work most efficiently in Windows, you should use a mouse. You can press mouse buttons and move the mouse in various ways to change the way it performs:

Point means to move the mouse pointer onto the specified item by moving the mouse. The tip of the mouse pointer must be touching the item.

Click on an item means to move the pointer onto the specified item and press the mouse button once. Unless otherwise specified, use the left mouse button.

Double-click on an item means to point at the specified item and press and release the mouse button twice quickly.

Drag means to move the mouse pointer onto the specified item, hold down the mouse button, and move the mouse while holding down the button.

Appendix A

You can use the mouse to perform common Windows activities, including running applications and moving and resizing windows.

Starting a Program

To start a program, simply double-click on its icon (or Tab to it and press Enter). If its icon is contained in a program group window that's not open at the moment, open the window first. Follow these steps:

1. If necessary, open the program group window that contains the program you want to run. To open a program group window, click on its icon.

2. Double-click on the icon for the program you want to run.

Using Menus

The pull-down menu bar (see Figure A.2) contains various menus from which you can select commands. Each Windows program that you run has a set of pull-down menus; Windows itself has a set, too.

To open a menu, click on its name on the menu bar. Once a menu is open, you can select a command from it by clicking on the desired command.

What Are Accelerator keys? Notice that in Figure A.2, some commands are followed by key names, such as Enter (for the **O**pen command) or F8 (for the **C**opy command). These are called *accelerator keys*. You can use these keys to perform these commands without even opening the menu.

Windows Basics   133

Usually, when you select a command, the command is performed immediately. However:

- If the command name is gray (rather than black), the command is unavailable at the moment and you cannot choose it.

- If the command name is followed by an arrow, selecting the command will cause another menu to appear, from which you select another command.

- If the command name is followed by an ellipsis (three dots), selecting it will cause a dialog box to appear. You'll learn about dialog boxes in the next section.

Navigating Dialog Boxes

A dialog box is Windows' way of requesting additional information. For example, if you choose **Print** from the **File** menu of the Write application, you'll see the dialog box shown in Figure A.3.

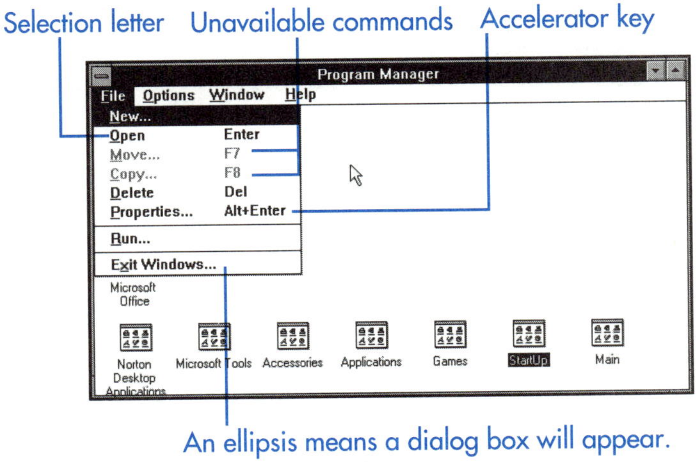

Selection letter   Unavailable commands   Accelerator key

An ellipsis means a dialog box will appear.

Figure A.2   A menu lists various commands you can perform.

Appendix A

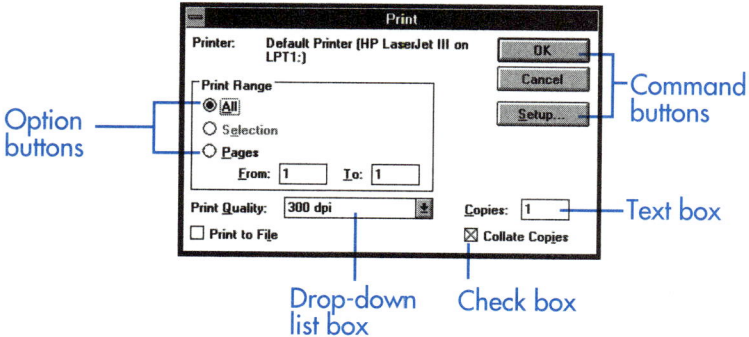

Figure A.3 A typical dialog box.

Each dialog box contains one or more of the following elements:

- *List boxes* display available choices. To activate a list, click inside the list box. If the entire list is not visible, use the scroll bar to view the items in the list. To select an item from the list, click on it.

- *Drop-down lists* are similar to list boxes, but only one item in the list is shown. To see the rest of the items, click on the down-arrow to the right of the list box. To select an item from the list, click on it.

- *Text boxes* allow you to type an entry. To activate a text box, click inside it. To edit an existing entry, use the arrow keys to move the cursor, and the Del or Backspace keys to delete existing characters, and then type your correction.

- *Check boxes* allow you to select one or more items in a group of options. For example, if you are styling text, you may select Bold and Italic to have the text appear in both bold and italic type. Click on a check box to activate it.

- *Option buttons* are like check boxes, but you can select only one option button in a group. Selecting one button unselects any option that is already selected. Click on an option button to activate it.

- *Command buttons* execute (or cancel) the command once you have made your selections in the dialog box. To press a command button, click on it.

Switching Between Windows

Many times, you will have more than one window open at once. Some open windows may be program group windows, while others may be actual programs that are running. To switch among them, you can:

- Pull down the Window menu, and choose the window you want to view.

OR

- If a portion of the desired window is visible, click on it.

Controlling A Window

As you saw earlier in this appendix, you can minimize, maximize, and restore windows on your screen. But you can also move them and change their size.

- To move a window, drag its title bar to a different location. (Remember, "drag" means to hold down the left mouse button while you move the mouse.)

- To resize a window, position the mouse pointer on the border of the window until you see a double-headed arrow; then drag the window border to the desired size.

Index

Symbols

3-D gray dialog boxes, 109

A

About Organizer command (Help menu), 13
accelerator keys (Windows), 131
adding
  anniversaries to Anniversary section, 87-88
  entries to phone logs, 80
  events to Planner, 63
  tasks to To Do lists, 47-49
Address command (Options menu), 73
Address section, 4, 66-67
  adding addresses, 68-70
  changing views, 67-70
  deleting addresses, 70
  exporting addresses, 78-79
  finding addresses quickly, 71-72
  importing addresses, 74-77
  order of sorting, 72
  searching records, 68

address templates, 66
Alarm dialog box, 36
alarms for appointments, 36-38
anchor icon, 117
Anniversary section, 4, 86
  adding to/deleting from, 87-90
  correcting entries, 88-89
applications
  linking files, 121-123
  running at preset time with Calendar, 38-39
appointment window, 28, 36
appointments
  assigning costs, 40
  deleting, 30
  Disappearing Duration Time, 35
  duration, 33-34
  editing text, 28-29
  length/time, 32
  time of, 34-35
  rescheduling, 29-30
  setting alarms, 36-38
  setting with Calendar section, 27-28
ASCII text files, importing, 75
assigning
  confidential status to tasks, 49
  costs to appointments, 40

Autodialer, 110, 114-115
Autodialer command (Options menu), 114

B

Baud rates, Autodialer phone calls, 114
binders, colors, 106-107
bitmaps, Notepad, 55
blank pages, Notepad, 55
BMP file name extensions (bitmap files), 55
Browse button, 38
Bubble help, 11
buttons
   Alarm, 36
   Browse, 38
   Cost Codes, 40
   Link, 117
   Run Program, 38
   Windows, Minimize/Maximize/ Restore, 129

C

Calendar
   customizing, 42-44
   running applications at preset time, 38-39
   viewing information in Planner, 64-65
Calendar section, displaying entries from other sections, 45-46
Calendar command (Options menu), 42
Calendar Options (Show) dialog box, 45
Calendar section, 4, 23-24
   setting appointments, 27-28
   turning pages, 25-26
Call Log dialog box, 82
cancelling appointments, 30
CD \WINDOWS command, 1, 128

changing
   page layout setup, 97-99
   passwords, 103-105
   charts in Planner, changing views, 62
clicking items with mouse, 130
Clipboard
   DDE (Dynamic Data Exchange), 56
   pasting graphics into Notepad, 58
colors of binders, 106-107
combining file sections, 20-22
commands
   CD \WINDOWS, 1, 128
   Edit menu
      Paste, 59
      Search, 71
      Undo, 31
   File menu
      Exit, 5
      Export, 78
      Import, 75
      New, 16
      Open, 19
      Page Setup, 96
      Passwords, 102
      Print, 91
      Printer Setup, 94
      Reference, 121
      Save, 17
      Save As, 17-18
   Help menu, 12-13
      About Organizer, 13
      Commands, 13
      Exit, 15
      How Do I?, 13
      Index, 12
      Shortcuts, 13
      Using Help, 13
   Options menu
      Address, 73
      Autodialer, 114
      Calendar, 42

Customize, 20
  Display, 107
  Notepad, 57
  Planner, 64
  Preferences, 108
  Page menu, Next Page/Prior
    Page, 89
  selecting in Windows, 131
  Tools menu
    Phone Call, 110
    Phone Log, 112
    SmartIcons, 9
  WIN, 1
compacting files, 126-127
Completed dialog box, 50
confidential status, assigning to
  tasks, 49
context-sensitive Help, 11
correcting entries in Anniversary
  section, 88-89
Cost Codes dialog box, 40
costs to appointments, assigning, 40
CSV file name extension, 126
Ctrl+V keys (Paste command), 59
Customize command (Options
  menu), 20
Customize SmartIcon, 20
customizing
  Calendar, 42-44
  Notepad table of contents, 57
  Organizer preferences, 108-109
  Organizer screen, 106

D

damaged files, repairing, 124-126
databases, fields in records, 66
Date display, 24
DDE (Dynamic Data Exchange),
  Clipboard, 56
default duration time, 34
deleted tasks, retrieving, 52
deleting
  addresses, 70
  anniversaries, 89-90

appointments, 30
Notepad pages, 59
tasks from To Do lists, 51-52
dialog boxes
  Address Options, 73
  Alarm, 36
  Anniversary, 87
  Autodialer Options, 114
  Calendar Options, 43
  Calendar Options (Show), 45
  Call Log, 82
  Completed, 50
  Cost Codes, 40
  Customize Organizer, 20
  Dial, 81, 110
  Display, 107
  Export, 78
  Field Mapping, 76
  File Open, 19
  File Save As, 17
  Font Mapping, 100
  Gray, 109
  Import, 75
  Include From, 21
  Include Section, 21
  Lotus Organizer Utilities, 125
  Notepad Options, 57
  Notepad Page Edit, 58
  Notepad Page Insert, 54
  Notes, 85
  Paper Layouts, 96
  Passwords, 102
  Phone Log, 83, 112
  Planner Options, 64
  Preferences, 108
  Print, 91
  Reference, 121
  Run Program, 38
  Search, 14, 71
  Status, 125
  To Do, 48
  Tools SmartIcons, 9
  Windows, 132-134

directories
  \ORGANIZE\SAMPLE, Planner section, 61
  Windows, switching to, 1
disabling dialing options, 82
disappearing duration time, 35
Display command (Options menu), 107
displaying entries from other sections in Calendar section, 45-46
double-clicking with mouse, 130
down-arrow icon, 28
drag-and-drop method of changing appointments, 29
dragging with mouse, 130
duration of appointments, changing, 33-34

E

Edit menu commands
  Paste, 59
  Search, 71
  Undo, 31
editing appointment text, 28-29
entries, adding to phone logs, 80
events, adding to Planner, 63
Exit command (File menu), 5, 15
Exit SmartIcon, 5
Export command (File menu), 78
exporting addresses, 78-79
external links, 122

F

F1 key (Help), 11
Field Mapping dialog box, 76
fields in database records, 66
File menu commands
  Exit, 5, 15
  Export, 78
  Import, 75
  New, 16
  Open, 19

Page Setup, 96
Passwords, 102
Print, 91
Printer Setup, 94
Reference, 121
Save, 17
Save As, 17-18
file name extensions
  BMP (bitmap files), 55
  CSV, 126
  WMF (Metafiles), 55
files, 16
  ASCII text, importing, 75
  combining sections, 20-22
  compacting, 126-127
  CSV, 126
  importing addresses from, 74
  linking from other applications, 121-123
  opening, 18-20
  Organizer, 4
  repairing damaged, 124-126
  SAMPLE.ORG, 61
  saving, 16-17
Font Mapping dialog box, 100
fonts, 99-101

G-H

graphics, pasting into Notepad pages, 58-59
Gray dialog boxes, 109
guidelines, selecting passwords, 102

hanging-up modems, 82
Help, 11-12
  menu commands, 12-13
    About Organizer, 13
    Commands, 13
    How Do I?, 13
    Index, 12
    Shortcuts, 13
    Using Help, 13
  SmartIcon, 11

Index

I-K

icons
    anchor, 117
    down-arrow, 28
    Last Name view, Address
        section, 68
    Link, 119
    Lotus Applications program
        group, 2
    Phone, 110
    Print, 91
    Program Manager, 1
    Run Program, 39
    Trash, 30
    Unfold, 62
    View, Calendar section, 25
Import command (File menu), 75
importing addresses, 74-77
Include From dialog box, 21
Include Section dialog box, 21
Index command (Help menu), 12

jump words, 12

L

labels, printing, 93-95
Last Name view icon, Address
    section, 68
length/time of appointments, 32
Link button, Toolbox, 117
Link menu, 120
links, 116
    multiple, 119-120
    Notepad, 55
    to other application files, 121-123
logging phone calls, 80-85
Lotus Applications program group
    icon, 2
Lotus Organizer
    quitting, 5
    screen components, 2-4
    sections, 4-5
    starting, 1-2
Lotus Organizer Utilities dialog box, 125

M

making phone calls with
    Autodialer, 110-112
managing tasks on To Do lists, 50-51
menus, Windows, 131-132
Metafiles, Notepad, 55
Microsoft Windows, see Windows
Minimize/Maximize buttons
    (Windows), 129
modems
    Autodialer phone calls, 114
    hanging-up, 82
mouse, using in Windows, 129-130
moving windows, 134
multiple days, scheduling in
    Planner, 63
multiple links, 119-120

N

names, placing on Organizer, 106
New command (File menu), 16
New File SmartIcon, 16
Next Page command (Page
    menu), 89
Notepad command (Options
    menu), 57
Notepad Page Edit dialog box, 58
Notepad Page Insert dialog box, 54
Notepad pages
    creating, 53-56
    deleting, 59
    pasting graphics into, 58-59
Notepad section, 4, 53
Notes dialog box, 85

O

Open command (File menu), 19
opening files, 18-20
options for printing, 95
Options menu commands
    Address, 73
    Autodialer, 114
    Calendar, 42

Customize, 20
Display, 107
Notepad, 57
Planner, 64
Preferences, 108
order of sorting, Address section, 72
\ORGANIZE\SAMPLE directory, Planner section, 61
Organizer
    customizing screen, 106
    files, 4
    page layout setup, 96-97
    personalizing, 106
    preferences, 108-109
    printing sections, 91-93
Organizer Utilities, 124

P

page layout setup, 96-99
Page menu commands, Next Page/Prior Page, 89
Page Setup command (File menu), 96
page views, Calendar, 44
pages
    Notepad, 53-56
    deleting in Notepad, 59
    turning in Calendar section, 25-26
paper white monitors, 107
passwords, 102-105
Passwords command (File menu), 102
Paste command (Edit menu), 59
Paste SmartIcon, 59
pasting graphics into Notepad pages, 58-59
personalizing Organizer, 106
Phone Call command (Tools menu), 110
phone calls
    logging, 80-83
    making with Autodialer, 110-112
    speed dialing, 111
    tracking logged, 83-85
Phone Log command (Tools menu), 112
Phone Log dialog box/SmartIcon, 83
phone logs
    adding entries to, 80
    reviewing, 112-113
Planner
    adding events, 63
    changing views, 62
    viewing Calendar information, 64-65
Planner command (Options menu), 64
Planner section, 4, 60-61
Pointer tool, Toolbox, 119
pointing mouse, 130
ports, 114
preferences
    Autodialer, 114-115
    Organizer, 108-109
Preferences command (Options menu), 108
Print command (File menu), 91
Printer Setup command (File menu), 94
printing
    fonts, 99
    labels, 93-95
    options, 95
    Organizer sections, 91-93
Prior Page command (Page menu), 89
Program Manager, Windows, 130
Program Manager window, 1
programs, starting, 131

Q-R

Quick dial list box, Autodialer, 112
quitting Lotus Organizer, 5

read only passwords, 102
records, 66

Index

Reference command (File menu), 121
removing tasks from To Do lists, 51-52
repairing damaged files, 124-126
repositioning SmartIcon palette, 9-10
rescheduling appointments, 29-30
resizing windows, 134
Restore button (Windows), 129
retrieving deleted tasks, 52
reviewing phone logs, 112-113
Run Program dialog box, 38
running applications at preset time with Calendar, 38-39

S

SAMPLE.ORG file, 61
Save As command (File menu), 17-18
Save command (File menu), 17
Save SmartIcon, 17
saving
　damaged files, 124-126
　files, 16-17
scheduling multiple days in Planner, 63
screens
　Organizer
　　components, 2-4
　　customizing, 106
　Windows
　　components, 128-129
　　title, 128
Search command (Edit menu), 71
Search feature, 13-15
Search SmartIcon, 71
searching Address section records, 68
section tabs, 4
sections
　Address, 66-67
　Anniversary, 86
　Calendar, 23-24

Lotus Organizer, 4-5
Notepad, 53
Planner, 60-61
printing, 91
To Do list, 47
setting
　appointments with Calendar section, 27-28
　Autodialer preferences, 114-115
　links, 117-119
Shortcuts command (Help menu), 13
SmartIcon palette, 9-10
SmartIcons
　Customize, 20
　Exit, 5
　Help, 11
　New File, 16
　Paste, 59
　Phone Log, 83
　Save, 17
　Search, 71
　Undo, 31
SmartIcons command (Tools menu), 9
sorting orders, Address section, 72
speed dialing phone calls, 111
starting
　Lotus Organizer, 1-2
　programs, 131
　Windows, 128
Status dialog box, 125
switching among windows, 134
switching to Windows directory, 1

T

tables of contents, Notepad, 57-58
tasks
　adding to To Do lists, 47-49
　assigning confidential status, 49
　managing on To Do lists, 50-51
　removing from To Do lists, 51-52
　retrieving deleted, 52

templates for addresses, 66
text of appointments, editing, 28-29
Time Display, 4
time of appointments, changing, 34-35
TimeTracker, 32-33
To Do dialog box, 48
To Do list section, 4, 47
To Do lists
    adding to, 47-49
    deleting from, 51-52
    managing, 50-51
Today's Date, 4
Toolbox, 3
    Link button, 117
    Pointer tool, 119
    Print icon, 92
Tools menu commands
    Phone Call, 110
    Phone Log, 112
    SmartIcons, 9
tracking costs against appointments, 39
tracking logged phone calls, 83-85
Trash, 4, 30
turning pages in Calendar section, 25-26

U

Undelete utilities, 18
Undo command (Edit menu), 31
Undo SmartIcon, 31
Unfold icon, 62
Using Help command (Help menu), 13
utilities
    Autodialer, 110
    Organizer, 124
    Undelete, 18

V

View icon palette, 4
View icons, Calendar section, 25
views
    Address, 67-70
    Calendar pages, 44
    Planner, 62

W-Z

WIN command, 1
Windows
    command selection, 131
    dialog boxes, 132-134
    menus, 131-132
    Minimize/Maximize/Restore button, 129
    starting, 128
    using mouse, 129-130
windows
    appointment, 28, 36
    Help, 13
    Lotus Applications group, 2
    moving, 134
    Program Manager, 1
    resizing, 134
    switching among, 134
Windows directory, switching to, 1
Windows Program Manager, 130
Windows screen components, 128-129
WMF file name extensions (Metafiles), 55

10 Minutes is all you need to begin learning about:

10 Minute Guide to Excel 5
ISBN: 1-56761-321-7
Softbound, $10.95 USA

10 Minute Guide to Lotus 1-2-3, Rel. 4 for Windows
ISBN: 1-56761-034-x
Softbound, $10.95 USA

10 Minute Guide to MS-DOS 6.2
ISBN: 1-56761-416-7
Softbound, $10.95 USA

10 Minute Guide to Windows 3.1
ISBN: 0-672-30052-4
Softbound, $10.95 USA

10 Minute Guide to WordPerfect 6 for Windows
ISBN: 1-56761-133-8
Softbound, $10.95 USA

10 Minute Guide to Word for Windows 6
ISBN: 1-56761-345-4
Softbound, $10.95 USA

For the complete line of *10 Minute Guides*, check your favorite computer book retailer or call 1-800-428-5331 for a catalog and more information.